Beyond Chocolate

understanding Swiss culture

Margaret Oertig-Davidson

With best wishes,

Margot Oertig

Bergli

books

Beyond Chocolate
understanding Swiss culture

This edition published in 2006 by
Bergli Books   Tel.: +41 61 373 27 77
Rümelinsplatz 19   Fax: +41 61 373 27 78
CH-4001 Basel   e-mail: info@bergli.ch
Switzerland   www.bergli.ch

ISBN 3-905252-06-6

Beyond Chocolate
understanding Swiss culture

Welcome to the party

When you move to a new country you notice pretty quickly that things are different, but it can take a long time to figure out why. My idea in writing this book was to 'host a dinner party' for people who have made their home in Switzerland and want to meet people and hear stories which would help them understand the local culture and people. What combination of people would I invite to dinner to pass on their impressions and insights on different subjects? This is the answer I came up with: Swiss and foreign guests, that is, intercultural couples (foreigners with Swiss partners), employees of large international companies as well as small local ones, human resource managers, communication specialists, parents, educators and psychologists.

To narrow down the range of topics to be discussed, foreigners have mostly been chosen from a variety of westernised English-speaking countries related by history:[1] The USA, Canada, Britain, Ireland, Australia, New Zealand and South Africa. Most guests live in the German-speaking part of the country, but there are several comments and stories from the French and Italian speaking parts too. You will also spot a few German guests with an interesting perspective.

Some guests appear under their own name and others are slightly disguised at their own request, so that they can comment more freely. Many do not make an official appearance at all, but their views greatly influenced the direction of the discussion. My thanks go to them all for their willingness to share their experiences, insights and wisdom. A very special guest is Ariane Curdy,[2] a Swiss-French intercultural specialist based in Geneva, who grew up in Basel and worked for an international humanitarian organisation in Geneva for 14 years. Her insights are interspersed throughout the book.

This book invites you to join in a fairly serious discussion with people who like to talk about getting on with others, who think about why people behave the way they do, and who want to get past thinking about culture in terms of who is right and who is wrong. Cultures are systematic and there is a reason for everything you encounter. Hearing the accounts of others may give you a starting point to help you understand your own experiences of Switzerland and put them into perspective. The most important topics are repeated in different chapters, discussed from different angles, so that you can dip in to the subjects which you find most relevant, and leave the rest without missing out on the key issues.

As at any other party, you don't just believe everything you hear. People have to generalise in order to be able to express their opinions. You will form your own opinions about what you have heard, and adjust those opinions as you experience the variations in culture for yourself. No one, Swiss or foreign, who has read the draft of this book agrees with it all. Hopefully some readers will be prompted to continue the discussion and write their own books.

You may catch a hint of pain, which can later turn to amusement, as people describe bumping into 'coconut shells' or 'peach kernels'. Having your value system challenged by the assumptions and values of others is at the heart of intercultural experiences all over the world, and adjustment can involve discomfort in the beginning. It is my hope that the experiences and insights shared will help you make the adjustment more smoothly, and that you will find a comfortable place on your own personal interface between cultures.

Enjoy the party!

Margaret Oertig-Davidson

Section one: What's it all about?

Chapter 1 The peach and the coconut

Switzerland is not Sweden

Swiss people often comment that when they are travelling in the USA, some of the people they meet do not know the difference between Switzerland and Sweden. They both begin with 'S' and they both have snow in winter. Many British people coming to Switzerland categorise it vaguely in their minds as 'northern European' and expect it to be like the Netherlands or Scandinavia. Others have no preconceptions about Switzerland at all because they assume that deep down people are just the same, all over the world. As Professor K. O'Sullivan, an Australian linguist said, 'Australians think people everywhere are basically Australian'.[3] He contrasts this with the Chinese who tend to believe that non-Chinese differ from the Chinese in a way that is almost impossible to overcome. So if you scratch the surface of Swiss culture and attitudes, will you find people like yourself on a deeper level, or will you find Swiss people who differ from you 'in a way that is impossible to overcome'? How you answer that question depends on your own background, your particular way of relating to people and who you meet in Switzerland. This book should help you

The main focus of the book is on certain issues which are relevant to people from a variety of westernised English-speaking countries. This does not mean that Americans, Canadians, Irish and New Zealanders are the same, or that they all experience Switzerland in the same way in all respects. Even within one of these countries there are enormous differences in cultures and subcultures. Dan Daniels, an American professor in Switzerland, points out that there are major differences in the US among such groups as southern white Protestants, north eastern Catholics, big-city African-Americans, west coast Asians and Rocky Mountain Native Americans. Most of the people expressing their views in the book are white, middle-class, from college-educated cultures with some religious spread. An attempt to describe the ways in which English speakers in the USA and around the world may differ from each other is not within the scope of this book.

along your way, by pointing out some of the underlying Swiss values which may play a role in your everyday life.

The name game

Superficial observations can help confirm something you already assumed about a country. For instance, when you experience the excellent public transport system, it confirms your assumptions about Swiss efficiency (see also chapter 23). Some observations are more difficult to understand. When I started teaching English in Switzerland, the school staff called me Frau Oertig. I found it quite entertaining because I had never been called by my surname before. In professional situations in Scotland people ei-

Change - change back

In the Swiss workplace, staff may use first names solely for the benefit of a native speaker of English. Swiss, Alsatian French and German staff in Basel often use each others' surnames when speaking German in the office but change to first names with their whole team when speaking English in the presence of a visitor from the United States or Britain. Once she or he has gone and they are speaking German again, they change back. If English-speaking staff come to work in their department more long term, they may change permanently to first names.

ther said 'Margaret' or didn't say my name at all. In the Swiss classroom I used students' first names if possible. One intermediate group was a bit resistant, and when I said 'What's your name?' they said things like 'Meier' and 'Niederberger'. I then patiently told them in slow, clear English that I was called Margaret and asked them again what their names were. I managed to get their first names out of them. After I had been having classes with them for a couple of years, we went out for a drink together and I was very surprised when they started clinking their wine glasses and re-introducing themselves to each other. Some of them just said things like, 'I'm Doris' which seemed a bit pointless to me as we all knew that already. Others suddenly had shorter names. The man who had told me his name was Niklaus was now 'Niggi'.

What they were actually doing was observing the Swiss custom of taking the opportunity to change over from the more formal use of surnames to the more intimate use of first names over a drink. In the classroom I had initiated this prematurely and although they had gone along with it (in their adaptable Swiss way), they still felt the need of the ritual to do it properly. Niklaus had been a useful cover to offer people like me, who insisted on calling him by his first name before he was ready. With his friends he used the dialect form, 'Niggi'.

The peach and the coconut

It took me a long time to appreciate the deeper significance of using first names or surnames in Switzerland. Intercultural trainers working in a German-speaking environment often use the example of the peach and the coconut to help clarify these attitudes to relationships. This idea is thought to have been developed from a distinction made by Kurt Lewin,[4] a German-American psychologist who was interested in the boundaries of the public and private 'life spaces' of Germans and Americans. In the diagram of the coconut and peach on the next page, the outer layer of the fruit represents the person's public space and the inner layer, their private space.

In Switzerland as in Germany and many other European and Asian cultures, there is traditionally a coconut culture. In the coconut model, people make a clear distinction between their neighbours, colleagues and acquaintances in the outer layer, and their family and friends in the inner layer. They typically use surnames in the outer layer and first names in the inner layer. In the outer layer they may not wish to give personal information about them-

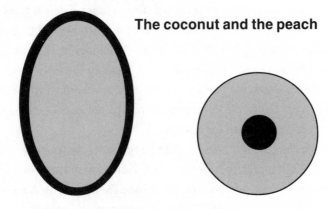

The coconut and the peach

selves to others. Symbolically they have a larger private space in the inner layer because they share more about themselves there, with people they know very well. Their homes are part of their private sphere and they are unlikely to entertain guests they hardly know in them. Once people have moved into the inner layer, the commitment is long-term.

The peach model is found increasingly in English-speaking cultures and makes particular sense to highly mobile people of various nationalities. They do not make such a clear distinction between friends and non-friends in the outer layer, the flesh of the peach. They may share a lot of themselves and behave in a relaxed, friendly manner towards a wider range of people. They sometimes treat new people (who are in fact strangers) as potential friends, talking to them openly and personally, as if they have already known them a while. This lack of a clear distinction is also reflected in the preference for using first names with everyone, so that there is no obvious barrier to getting closer. Their homes are part of their public sphere and they are comfortable inviting people home when they hardly know them. The inner layer is small in contrast, usually the family, which is possibly the only group of people with whom they will maintain a close relationship for their whole lives. Other close relationships are not necessarily long-term. You can be close for a while.

While the coconut is thought to be typically Swiss or German, and the peach typically American, individuals may vary quite a bit, according to their personality. Lawrence Desmond, an American anthropologist, also points out that there are also cultures in the USA which may be less peach and more coconut.

> Peach in coconut country
> Rosemary is British and lives in a village in the French part of Switzerland. When she got a new neighbour, they started walking their dogs together. Rosemary chatted freely about herself, her family and her job. Madame Perret, her neighbour, volunteered very little information about herself and so Rosemary asked her about her job. Madame Perret answered very briefly that she was a physiotherapist. She seemed reluctant to say more, and Rosemary decided not to press for more details. Later in passing, Madame Perret mentioned that she had to dress lightly because it was so hot in the hospital where she worked. If this information was not a secret, why did she not reveal it earlier when Rosemary asked her about her job? To Rosemary it would make the conversation flow more easily. To her neighbour, more time was needed before she would want to start talking about personal matters.

For Rosemary as a peach person, the hard layer was experienced at the beginning, when Madame Perret was not ready to let her in to a range of areas of her life. Culture and personality can both play a role.

Coconut in peach country

Swiss and Germans often report experiences in peach countries which leave them thinking people there are 'superficial'. Monika is German and studied in England. There she found people used the word 'friend' very frequently. People who travelled on the bus together were 'friends', and some students did not even know the surname of their friends. People often seemed very friendly, and said, 'you must come round for a cup of tea', but then no concrete invitation followed. Coming from a 'coconut country', she took it seriously when someone said they wanted to invite her to their house. To her it was a sign of initiating real friendship, and she was disappointed when nothing came of it.

For Monika, (see above) a peach person talking personally and issuing an invitation was giving out signals of being a friend, and seemed to be making a commitment. When Monika then discovered the peach person had no real commitment to her, she was disappointed and considered the person superficial.

Swiss friends

To understand the meaning of friendships on the inner layer of the coconut, take a look at the following comments of English speaking foreigners in Switzerland who have experienced a 'coconut' relationship. It is striking how often the word 'friend' is connected with loyalty and trust in their comments. Here are some examples:

· 'I think most Swiss are honest, and loyal (once you are privileged to be their friend)'. *Ellen (American)*

· 'On a personal level we found that once a true friendship had been established (which may take a little while), it was definitely for the long term and characterised by total trust.' *Erik (English)*

· 'What I like best about the Swiss people: Their honesty, their correctness, their loyalty, their lack of super ficiality, and once one is considered a friend by them they will be a friend for life in return'. *Lucy (English)*

· 'I like the loyalty and thoughtfulness friends have towards their friends'. *Sharon (American)*

· 'Once you get to know them, they are caring and loyal'. *Sandra (American)*

Do you shake hands or kiss?

Joyce is from the USA and has noticed over the years that in the German-speaking part of the country, kissing people on the cheek can be a symbol of the relationship inside the coconut:

In my daughter's kindergarten class, all the parents agreed to say *Du* to each other and use first names, and this created a relaxed, friendly atmosphere. However I now realise there is a big difference in the relationship between using first names and shaking hands and using first names and kissing. I got on great with some of the other mothers and one day I had a good talk in the park with one woman, Martha, sharing feelings while our kids played. I spontaneously kissed her on the cheek when it was time to leave. This changed our relationship. For Martha, kissing goodbye was a sign of moving into a deeper commitment I had not actually meant to convey. After that, she expected us to get together more often. Now when I see her, I will always feel obliged to kiss her on the cheek, even if our relationship becomes less close.

For Martha, Joyce's spontaneous gesture was symbolic of moving into a deeper relationship. For Joyce, at that moment, she felt very warmly towards her, but that did not mean that Martha had graduated to becoming one of her close friends.

The long-term approach to friendship

It is hard to overlook the importance of the time factor in the comments on Swiss friendship. Swiss people tend to think long-term, and friendships take time to grow. There are reasons for this, connected with people's attitudes to their roots.

In Switzerland people have great respect for their place of origin, and feel they belong there. They are much less likely to want to change region than people from many English speaking cultures. Each canton is like another country in many ways, and people make jokes about the people in other cantons and imitate each other's dialects. German and Italian-speaking Swiss are proud of their regional dialects which stay with them all their lives, even when they move away, while the French-speaking Swiss have a different accent from the French but rarely speak a dialect of French.[5] (See chapter 6 for more information on languages and dialects in Switzerland).

> **All over the place**
> Recently I met Jean, from the USA, at a conference. 'Where are you from?' I asked. 'All over the place really,' she replied. 'As my brother always jokes, when we were old enough to walk, we left Arkansas, and when we were old enough to drive, we left Texas'. This struck me as quite a different attitude. Very few people in Switzerland are from 'all over the place' and it would be unheard of for a Swiss person to say, 'when we were old enough to walk we left Emmental and when we were old enough to drive we left Bern'. People would find it strange that the Emmentaler was not respectful of the place of his roots.

Heimatort

Heimatort is not a kind of cake, but rather the word German Swiss use for the community (town or village) from which their family originated. It can also be called their *Bürgerort*. In French it is the *lieu d'origine* and in Italian, *luogo di attinenza*. Swiss people inherit this place of origin from their father, and it is passed on through the generations. The *Heimatort* is written on their passport rather than their actual place of birth, although it may have been several generations since anyone in the family actually lived there. If you live in a village where lots of people have the same name, they are probably all still living in their *Heimatort*.

Christine is German Swiss and believes the *Heimatort* can be really important to Swiss people:
My Heimatort is Lenzburg, where my father grew up. I have never lived in Lenzburg, but as a child I visited my grandparents there. My husband and I had our civil wedding ceremony there and my father really emphasised in his wedding speech how much this meant to him.

A strong sense of roots affects the approach to friendship in Switzerland. Christine believes most Swiss people tend to prefer to stay where they grow up and only move away if they have to. True friendship is developed slowly over years, starting in kindergarten, school, or at the latest, during apprenticeships or tertiary education. The best friendships often go back to primary school, and recently a journalist, Sandra Studer, even referred to her best friend as her 'sandbox friend'. You know a person in quite a different way if you have been in and out of their house in childhood, getting to know their family too. There is a spontaneous intimacy at this stage of life, which in Switzerland is less likely to be repeated in adult life.

Students

From the Swiss point of view, a friend is almost like a brother or sister. Moving on to higher education does not necessarily mean people lose their previous school friends. Campus life is non-existent and many students live at home with their parents, or take a room in the university town and go home at weekends. They may initiate some new relationships but they will probably maintain the old relationships too.

> When Swiss students share an apartment, they are not just sharing the same accommodation for convenience, as is the case in more loosely structured 'peach' societies. They share their lives for a period and make a definite commitment to 'live together', and cook and eat together regularly. The German Swiss call it a *Wohngemeinschaft*, literally translated, a living community. If people do not want to enter into such a commitment, they rent a room with use of a kitchen and bathroom from a landlady (or *Schlummermutter*). There is not much in between.

Swiss young adults usually prefer to find work in the town where they were born and feel at home. During working life, as well as keeping their close friends, they often maintain long-term connections, which are known as *Seilschaften* (*Seil* means rope, as used in mountain tours). These ropes have certain similarities to the British idea of the 'old school tie' or the 'old boy network'. More is said about ropes and networks in chapter 22.

Short-term friendship

In many English-language communities, people use the word 'friend' loosely to describe people they meet in their free time. These are often highly mobile sub-cultures. To test your own mo-

Ariane Curdy is a French Swiss organization development and intercultural professional. Her consulting firm 'Ctrl Culture Relations' is based near Geneva.[2] She reports:

French Swiss are known for their cosmopolitan attitudes. Studies have revealed that more than two thirds of French Swiss top managers have more than one year's experience of working abroad, whereas in the USA only one-third of the CEOs have ever worked abroad. Switzerland's being so small promotes the urge to see the outside world (whereas many Americans move ... but remain within their own country).

I can also see many youngsters here who don't necessarily stay in their birthplace to study or work. Two of my French-speaking cousins left their village in the Valais region, first to go and learn German in Germany. This is a frequent practice, since it is in your interest to also speak German if you want to have access to the best jobs in Switzerland.

bility history, stop reading for a moment and count how many communities you have lived in where you have made a new set of friends and colleagues. In the USA this kind of experience is common all across the country. According to The National Geographic Survey 2000[6] fewer than 16% of Americans have always lived within 30 miles (48 kilometres) of their current address. Americans move their residence once every five years on average. The people who move away more than 30 miles are starting from scratch each time in developing their relationships at home and work.

According to the USA statistics, 16% of the US population have never moved more than 30 miles (48 kilometres) away. By Swiss standards, 48 kilometres is quite a distance. In Switzerland, you only have to move to the next village to be considered mobile. Swiss mobility statistics[7] report that in 1990 30.3% of the population of Switzerland still lived in the community (i.e. town or village) where they were born. In Basel it was 39.1%, in Bern 34.6%, St Gallen 33.9%, Zurich 33.1%, Lausanne 28% and Geneva 27%. Possibly more important than actual statistics is that Swiss people tend not to have such a 'mobility mentality'. They like to stay where they grew up.

It is assumed in many European countries that when people move a lot, their relationships are superficial, but short-term seems to me a more appropriate word. The relationships can be very deep and meaningful, but for logistical reasons it is hard to maintain them long-term. In Switzerland this is somehow a contradiction in terms. It is the long-term commitment, or the test of time which makes it a true friendship, not the fact that you connect well with a person over several months or a few years. A factor which leads to greater openness in mobile sub-cultures is that if you take risks and then regret it, you will probably be moving on anyway. If you live in the same neighbourhood all your life, you may be more wary of 'revealing all' because people may still remember your revelations 20 years later. You cannot reinvent yourself.

Ariane reports: In the French part, too, you differentiate between real, life-long friends, and more recent or professional acquaintances. But the Latins are much more extroverted, which fa-
vours a more 'peachy' attitude in certain circumstances.

I joined two different clubs in Geneva and Nyon recently.
With hardly any hesitation, people used first names and the informal *tu* and exchange of private information flowed naturally (with
some more than others, of course). In one club, a mechanic spontaneously volunteered to take care of my motorbike when he heard
I had serious troubles with it. At the other (sports) club, the tradition to bring a bottle along, and hang around together after the
working-out hours, emerged naturally. Some private events
emerged out of both clubs: a lunch with one member, a coffee with
another, and a garden party with all of them.

Peach-coconut hybrids

The peach and coconut models are merely useful simpli-
fications which provide a starting point for talking about a complex subject. It could be argued that there are many peach people
in coconut cultures and vice versa, or even as Mary from the USA
calls it, a fruit salad. Switzerland is changing fast, people are becoming more mobile (in 1960 38.1% of the total population lived
in the community they were born in, compared with 30.3% in
1990[8]) and the nature of relationships is changing with it, especially for the younger generation. The term 'fruit salad' may be
used to describe informal Swiss neighbourhoods where young

families get together, or a local sports club, where people are open to having relaxed relationships with a variety of new people. Where this is the case, the main difference which remains is that Swiss people would prefer to describe people in these relationships as colleagues, neighbours or acquaintances rather than friends. There is still a clear-cut distinction. Fellow club members will not necessarily visit each other in their homes, or share more personal details of their lives.

This book uses the expression 'German Swiss', 'French Swiss' and 'Italian Swiss' to describe Swiss people from the various linguistic regions, in the same way as you would say 'French Canadian' for a French-speaking person from Canada. 'Swiss German', 'Swiss French' and 'Swiss Italian' will be used when referring to the languages and dialects. (No one feels the need to say 'Romansch Swiss' or 'Swiss Romansch', as these people have a unique language they do not share with any other nation. 'Romansch' is enough). The translation of 'Deutsch-Schweizer' as 'German Swiss' (for the people) and 'Schweizer-Deutsch' as 'Swiss-German' (for the language/ group of dialects), is found in the Pons Collins dictionary (1997). It would be long-winded to say 'German-speaking Swiss', 'French-speaking Swiss' and 'Italian-speaking Swiss' every time they are mentioned, and they are mentioned very frequently.

Chapter 2   How people talk

It is a typical characteristic of peach cultures to talk to strangers as if they were friends. After I had been in Switzerland for a year or so, I overheard an English woman buying wine glasses in a shop, telling the shop assistant that they were for her Swiss hostess because it was her birthday. The assistant didn't seem to know what to reply, and I realised that it wasn't expected that customers would give personal information to a shop assistant they didn't know, even if the topics were directly related to what they were buying. It is easier to have chats in shops in small towns, where the assistants get to know customers over months and years.

Sue, an American woman who had just arrived in Switzerland, reported that it was easy to chat to locals when out walking her dog, but they seemed to be taken aback if she ventured away from the topic 'dog', or asked them their names. It was probably all going too fast for them. A degree of involvement has to be built up over time. Pat is Welsh and has lived in Switzerland for a few years. She now enjoys the relationships she has built up over the months and years while out walking her dog. She jokingly calls the people she chats to her *Hundeverein* (Dog club):

> Swiss people have a sincerity but a distance, which suits my temperament. I meet some other dog walkers again and again, and we talk about God and the world.

I once went into a bank in Scotland on Good Friday, and as she served me, the deputy manager told me that at first they had not been planning to open that day at all. She had made plans to visit her sister in England, and then her boss told her she had to come to work after all. It is quite funny to imagine a Swiss bank manager telling you this. It would not be considered professional.

Involvement and independence

In the conversations she initiated, Sue was not in step with the locals and neither was the English woman buying the glasses. In Sue's case, it probably just needed a few months of meeting the same people while out dog-walking for conversations to get going. In the case of people meeting in a shop in a city, there probably will be no relationship building up over time.

In any interaction (not only verbal) we are negotiating the degree to which we are involving the other person and the degree to which we are giving them space. How much we get involved depends on personality and gender as well as the type of culture we come from. Sue was quite extroverted and wanted to involve people in conversations beyond dog topics, but other dog owners felt their privacy was being threatened when they were asked to give more information about themselves to a stranger.

People from peach cultures generally have a greater desire to feel included and find something in common when they talk to others. Wanting to be liked is not uncommon either. In coconut cultures people have a greater desire to be given independence, space and respect. Being respected is more emphasised than being liked.

If both parties do not both want the same degree of involvement, a culture clash can occur in which they both lose face. In the world of sociolinguistics, 'face' can be defined as the public self-image that every member of society wants to claim for him or herself.[9] Although we do not want to behave in a way that threatens the face of others, we can easily do this if we are not aware of their 'face needs'.

The Hong Kong based cross-cultural communication specialists Scollon and Wong-Scollon describe the way people 'give' each other face as politeness strategies of involvement or independence.[10] They use these terms to compare the way people relate in the business world in the USA and Asian cultures respectively. At any given time people are using one strategy more than the other, although there may be a mix. Strategies of independence tend to be used more in public life in Switzerland than in English-speaking cultures, both in business and in the local community. Some key features of these different politeness strategies are outlined below:

Politeness strategies of involvement

(These are used in the outer layer of the peach. Some will also be used in the inner layer of the coconut).

- Paying attention to others
- Showing a strong interest in their affairs by asking questions
- Giving information about yourself
- Assuming you know something about others
- Trying to find out what you have in common
- Using first names
- Smiling at strangers and chatting to strangers as if they were friends (e.g. jokes, compliments)

Politeness strategies of independence

(These are used in the outer layer of the coconut)

- Not assuming you know anything about the others
- Not trying to find out either
- Finding small talk superficial or false (you don't mean it)
- Using silence as the highest level of independence
- Valuing correct behaviour more than friendly behaviour
- Using surnames to mark boundaries and show respect
- Observing rituals to show respect

In Switzerland people tend not to use strategies of involvement with people they do not know well, but there are exceptions. I found the childhood friends of my husband immediately very welcoming and open. I was considered part of the inside of the coco-

In workshops, Swiss people usually need an explanation of the involvement strategy 'assume you know something about others'. They cannot imagine doing this. An example might be to say to someone, 'I bet you could do with a coffee' or otherwise tell them how you think they feel.

nut, consisting of a particular in-group of school friends and their partners.

Another use of strategies of involvement with strangers is to 'chat them up'. Emma is American and reports that in her early days in Switzerland she once came back from a home visit to the USA resolving to be 'more herself', which for her meant chatting to people in the friendly way she would in the States:

The first guy I was friendly to followed me home. The wife of the second guy suddenly appeared defensively at his elbow as I admired his pullover. The third time I made sure I was more friendly to a woman, and that worked pretty well. It is better to talk to a stranger about his dog rather than about his pullover.

In a class, after I had introduced these politeness strategies, we happened to be discussing the 'polite' expression 'How can I help you?', sometimes used on the telephone. Ralf, who is German, identified the phrase as a typical strategy of involvement. He would think to himself, 'I don't need you to help me'.

Emma points out that you may be in negotiation with yourself as to how much you want to 'be yourself' in the new country, and that this process can go on for years.

You come across different politeness strategies in many professional situations. I used to enjoy flying out of Switzerland with British Airways because of the personal touch in the way they related to passengers. Recently I saw this more from a Swiss perspective when a BA flight attendant asked a passenger what he wanted to drink. 'Whisky with ice' said the man. 'Sounds good to me' replied the attendant as he reached for the whisky bottle. The flight attendant was expressing something they had in common, that he shared an appreciation for whisky. Swiss passengers may not see the point in finding something in common with people they meet in passing and will never see again. (They also do not feel the need to know the first names of staff).

The fact that fewer such personal comments are made by staff dealing with customers in German-speaking cultures means that English speakers may be tempted to describe Swiss people as 'cool'. With time, foreigners may re-interpret the Swiss 'coolness' (if it is polite) as professionalism and find that the more personal comments made by English-speaking staff about their cancelled holidays or drink preferences, etc., start to look inappropriate or even intrusive. Chapter 3 looks at the question of professional behaviour in more detail.

Chapter 3   It's not personal

Should you talk to clients and customers in the same casual way as you talk to friends? Or should they be treated with respectful distance? The coconut and peach models can also help account for differences in behaviour in the workplace. When I first came to Switzerland, I worked for two private language schools, both with mainly Swiss staff, but with very different 'company cultures'. In the large school with branches across the country, the staff were very polite and business-like and only spoke to me about matters strictly related to the classes. In the other smaller Basel-only school, we also chatted about the weather, new students, our hair-cuts, shopping, holidays, etc. There the staff and the school head were also more laid-back with the students. I was new to the country and felt more at home in the smaller school, but I now know that it would be considered less professional by many German Swiss service providers.

Being professional

An explanation of professional behaviour is given by Christine, who is German Swiss and works for a translation company which provides services to the banking sector in various Swiss cities. She defines it as follows:

> The main criterion is to be business-like and have the same relationship, whoever you speak to, and keep a professional distance. I always use surnames. If someone phones us, they are talking to a company. It shouldn't get personal. With Swiss clients it is more likely to get personal if something goes wrong or if it goes very well. Then emotions play a role. For example, if there is a very urgent order, and the client is very worried, and you manage to process it quickly, then they will praise you.

Christine is aware of differences between her approach to professionalism and the friendly style of foreigners.

> 'With foreigners it is a bit different. I was surprised when an American client phoned and told me in passing that she felt sick because she was pregnant. I did not discuss my pregnancy with any clients (most of whom never saw me anyway) until the day I left on maternity leave. Then I wrote an e-mail to them to let them know. There are foreign customers who are very laid-back. If an English speaker phones, I often need to ask, 'Who's speaking please?', because they don't give their name at the beginning of the call'.

Christine's description of professionalism fits with the politeness strategies of independence described in chapter 2, where some cultures show respectful distance towards people who are not close to them. As a service provider she finds this an important standard. While it is not 'the rule', as my example of the two schools shows, it is quite common. Giving too much personal information or asking personal questions may be considered unprofessional by some people.

Karin is Swiss and works for a Swiss bank, dealing with major clients and also defines professional as meaning 'not personal'. She believes staying calm and unemotional are important here too.

> Siegfried is German and grew up and worked in Switzerland for many years. In his current job as a chemist with ABB in England, he often has dealings with German companies.
>
> 'When my English team have meetings with German customers, they all use first names, which is okay in English. I use German customers' surnames, and they are very pleased about this. As fellow Germans, we all have the same understanding that first names symbolise you're a buddy, and this loses you a degree of respect and professional distance. Customers do not want to be my buddy'.

It's not about feelings

In international companies where people are working with colleagues of many nationalities, professionalism is not defined so precisely, and there can be quite a mix of politeness strategies. However, even German Swiss can feel uncomfortable when English-speaking colleagues make personal comments. Kathrin works for a bank and says the following:

> 'If I am complaining about something that has not been delivered, I find it very patronising if my English colleagues say things

to me like 'I can understand your frustration'. A Swiss colleague will keep things on a factual level and tell me the worst, or when I can expect delivery. He will not try to express my feelings for me'.

This reluctance to be personal can be a surprise to native English speakers, who are even used to advertisements which 'get personal'. As an example, in English language magazine advertisements for medication, there is frequent use of the word 'you' to address the reader personally over and over again, e.g. a US herbal product company which proclaims its 'commitment to making your herbal journey a rewarding one'. You are being led to believe the company is your friend and ally. This is a minor detail which helps give magazine readers the impression that they have friends everywhere. Advertisements in the German and Swiss German languages are more 'non-intrusive' in comparison, and may not so often address the matter of feelings. German Swiss would not buy into the idea of a company having a commitment to their herbal journey. (This book also uses the word 'you' frequently, to speak personally to the reader).

Compliments

When Sally taught English in England, her students from around the world often told her which of the lessons they really liked. When she started teaching in Switzerland she said the feedback and the compliments stopped, and she began to wonder if her teaching had gone downhill. It probably hadn't. In Switzerland, if you are qualified, it is assumed that you will do a good job. There is no need to make a big deal about it. People are not expected to make each other feel good, and are quick to interpret compliments as false flattery. This is quite different from the USA. The American writer Dale Carnegie's recipe for winning friends and influencing people was to make people feel important by flattering them sincerely. In Switzerland you should use compliments sparingly, and only when you really mean them. Janice is from the USA and comments that her Swiss husband will only accept a compliment from her if she backs it up with 'proof'.

Criticism is not personal

Anita is German Swiss and studied art in the USA. She found the approach to criticism quite different there than in Switzerland.

When we critiqued one another's paintings in the USA, we would very carefully point out all the positives, and then mention one negative, but very carefully. Now I'm studying at an art school in Switzerland. And man, that critique goes bam bam bam. In the USA feelings are taken very seriously. There you would rather start by talking about other things and slowly work up to the subject you actually want to discuss, to avoid hurting others' feelings. In Switzerland you come right to the point, and someone who comes from a different country will be offended, or hurt. Swiss people think, 'What does the point in question have to do with anyone's feelings? It is simply a technical matter. You don't lose time trying to avoid hurting feelings. Although people are not always successful in separating the technical information from feelings in Switzerland, it is usually the expectation that they should.

The reverse of this is described by Swiss people who have lived in the USA. The friendly American might be smiling and saying positive things for a long time, and it takes a while for the Swiss to realise the American is actually subtly criticising their work. Larry is American and comments that 'condemning with faint praise' is another technique used.

Ariane Curdy reports:

I came to similar conclusions about criticism while participating in a workshop in the United States. On the last day, eight people were asked to make a ten minutes presentation each. The audience were given evaluation sheets to qualify each performance with a "good" and "to be improved" column, and were asked to give oral feedback after each presentation. Suddenly I realised that the other participants were stressing the good points only, whereas I was quick in spotting and expressing the points to be improved, too. At the end, I almost felt like apologising, since I was aware that my Swiss feedback tradition might have hurt some feelings.

School practices

Practices with regard to criticism can be traced back to school. Beat is a Swiss manager and parent who has also lived with his family in the USA. He reports:

In the US people behave with more self confidence although they don't necessarily know a lot more than in Switzerland. Here in Swiss schools it is very hard to get all 6s (the top mark). The last few percent are hard to achieve and you never quite reach excellence. Even if the kids feel they have done well and fulfilled the expectations, up there is a teacher who knows a lot more and says your work is very good, but it's still not perfect. In the US, you have to do your work, but it's clear that if you do it well you get an A, the top grade.

Although many adults in Switzerland have experienced a tough marking system in the past, school is no longer like this across the country. In Basel City (Basel Stadt) schools, for example, teachers are generous with their praise, and pupils under 14 get test results and report cards which say they have 'more than met requirements', 'partially met requirements' or 'not yet met requirements'. This may influence the 'praise culture' of the future.

Being polite or matter-of-fact

Paolo is Ticinese (from the Italian-speaking part of Switzerland), but grew up in London. He is a teacher of English in Ticino, and says the following:

> I do not teach my Ticinese students the complex sentence structures you find in some English course books, like 'Do you think you could possibly . . .' or 'I hope you don't mind me saying so, but . . .' People in Ticino are not particularly loquacious and do not have much use for speaking indirectly. If someone opens the window on the train and there is a draught, the Ticinese who does not like the draught will either be shy and say nothing or tell them quite directly to close the window again.

There are clear parallels here with German Swiss communication preferences. German speakers also tend not to have much use for speaking indirectly, or manipulating the language in a complex way to ask for something. They identify that as 'very English'. If they have a right to ask, then they can ask directly.

Pointing out that people are doing something wrong should not be a personal matter. Marcel Trachsel compares the way people tell each other about the law:

> Below my office in Basel there is a one-way street. You often hear people yelling at drivers who are driving up it the wrong way. In Canada if someone wanted to tell me off for this, they would approach me with an apologetic look on their face and say politely, 'Excuse me, this is actually a one-way street'.

Canadians often add a personal touch to their message to soften it and save the face of the person being corrected. Thinking about the personal aspect of the interaction comes quite naturally in a peach culture, where people also relate to strangers and have little chats with them. (On the negative side, Larry, who is American, points out that in the USA it would be unwise to say anything because the other driver might have a gun). For German Swiss, reminding a stranger of the rules is not meant to be personalised communication. They know they are imposing (on the rule breaker's freedom), but limit the imposition by avoiding using any expressions which might suggest they are trying to relate personally to the rule breaker, as that would detract from the matter at hand. Clear, efficient communication should have higher priority.[11] The key issue is who is right, rather than how it is communicated.

One way to understand this direct approach is to treat it matter-of-factly, the way you look at a manufacturer's warning about how not to use their hair dryer. When you read 'DO NOT USE THIS HAIR DRYER IN THE BATH' you do not feel offended by it. You are glad to have been told. It would be inappropriate for the manufacturer to write 'We would really appreciate it if you did not take this hair dryer into the bath'. This conjures up a picture of a product team nervously wringing their hands at the idea of you in the bath with their hair dryer. But you do not want to think about the product team as you dry your hair. They minimise the intrusion by coming directly to the point efficiently with less personal interaction. It should be the same if you are driving the wrong way up a one-way street. You should be glad to have been told and do not need to consider the person who issued the warning.

The idea that correction is not meant personally is illustrated in the story of an American woman who put out both a Swiss flag and an American flag on her balcony after the September 11th attack on New York. Her Swiss neighbour pointed out to her that the American flag was higher than the Swiss one and that this wasn't acceptable (the American one was actually just bigger). The next day the neighbour returned with a lovely bunch of flowers to express her sympathy after the attack. The comment on the height of the flags was meant to be neutral information, and the flowers were a personal touch.

Telling it straight to customers

Straight talking has to be weighed up against feelings when talking to customers about technical matters. In communications training I sometimes present the following scenario and ask course participants to choose what to do from a variety of options:

You are a consultant called in to advise on upgrading a small company's computer system. You are surprised at how old-fashioned it is. Would you

a. Make it clear how old-fashioned it is?
b. Make positive comparisons between old and new to show them how much their lives are going to improve?
c. Make no reference to the present system and concentrate on advising on the update?

English speakers rarely choose (a) and say making a point of criticising the old system may offend the company. German Swiss who see the issue as one of technical expertise will tend to choose (a). Why not call a spade a spade, to let the client know what a difficult task you face, so that they then appreciate the miracles you do for them? Those Swiss staff with a strong customer orientation (which emphasises interpersonal skills more than technical issues) may go more for (b) so as not to offend. It also appears to vary from canton to canton, and German Swiss in the Basel area seem to be more willing to call a spade a spade than those in central Switzerland. A group of students in Lucerne told me this is because Basel is closer to the German border and, like the Germans, Basel people are more direct than people in the Lucerne area.

Those who emphasise technical aspects more than making the customer feel good may also argue that if you are not sure you can deliver something, it is better to tell people the worst so that they do not have their hopes raised and are then disappointed. Conscientious Swiss retailers and service providers may deal with clients in this way (see below).

No false promises

When I moved into my office I needed to have a phone installed but there was a delay because I hadn't been sent a phone number. After several phone calls over a period of a week, I finally spoke to an efficient call centre operator who promised to deal with it immediately. I was pretty annoyed about having waited so long and needed to hear things were moving at last. The last straw was when she said matter-of-factly, 'I'll deal with it today but I can't guarantee when it will arrive. It might take up to two weeks'. This was frustrating to hear but then only two days later, it suddenly arrived. A British operator would probably have reacted to my tone of frustration and reassured me with soothing promises like, 'it will probably arrive in a couple of days', even if she knew it could take longer.

Swiss staff are careful not to give people false hopes, and will not want that from you either. If you might be able to finish an urgent task between Wednesday and Friday, your Swiss customer will want to hear your most pessimistic estimate, which is Friday. Only say Wednesday if you are sure you can meet that deadline. Otherwise you will be considered unreliable. (See also chapter 25 on 'sticking to the plan'.)

Chapter 4   Correct behaviour

One autumn day I was sitting on the tram near three 13 or 14 year-old boys, who were going to the Herbstmesse, the Basel autumn fair. They were fooling around, hugging, pushing and shoving each other, and one even landed on my lap (and apologised to the woman next to me by mistake). Then a mother got on the tram with two toddlers, who started to wriggle about quite a bit on the full tram. The teenage boys stopped fighting and started to distract the little boys, chatting to them about the autumn fair and St Nicolas (Santa Claus) and then comparing the similar design of track shoes of one of the teenagers and one of the toddlers. When it was time to get off, all three boys shook hands with the two toddlers and said goodbye, then leapt off the tram.

I found the teenagers' behaviour quite intriguing. It seemed that they had switched roles from the 'younger ones' fooling around to the 'older ones' setting an example to the toddlers. (In Switzerland it is believed that the good example of adults is the main factor influencing children to grow up to be responsible members of society.) It was particularly interesting to me that after fooling around they shook hands with the young children, because I could not imagine young people in Britain switching behaviour in this way.

Issues like greeting people are mentioned many times in this book. Although these issues seem very superficial to English speakers, they are in fact indications of respect which German Swiss children learn at a young age when their basic values are falling into place. They are taught to say *Grüezi* to adults on the street and shake hands with the teacher when they go into kindergarten or school in the morning (but see also 'the *Hallo* virus' in chapter 21). In English-speaking countries children are taught not to talk to strangers and they do not shake hands with teachers.

In interviews for this book, British and Germans in particular referred to Swiss people being polite, and children were often mentioned too:

'I appreciate the general politeness. Children say 'Good morning' to strangers, which does not happen in Germany. In shops and offices people greet and thank each other and wish each other a good weekend. Young people are also very friendly and considerate, even punks'. *Christine (German)*

'What do I like most about Swiss people? Their civilness.' *Ken (Scottish)*

'I really love the Swiss people, and find them to be so very decent and mannerly and civilised'. *Lucy (English)*

'I find the people on the whole polite and respectful. They are sociable to you as a stranger, as long as you fit in with their behavioural rules'. *Helen (Scottish)*

There are many different words used here: polite, friendly, considerate, civilised, decent, mannerly, respectful, sociable. In German, another important word is *Anstand* which the dictionary defines as 'decency, propriety, good manners'. In Switzerland there is a ritual aspect to *Anstand* which is not clear from this German dictionary definition. It is not quite the same as good manners or politeness. I once asked some groups of (mostly) Swiss students of International Management at the University of Applied Sciences in Olten to contrast the two terms *Anstand* and politeness. They were in their early twenties, open-minded, fluent speakers of English, many of whom had lived and worked abroad. There were 35 people present, divided into seven groups for discussion. This is a summary of the salient points from their definitions:

> * *Anstand* is a basic code of behaviour, based on the unwritten rules of society. It is not optional if you don't want to 'break the rules'. It requires fairness, for example that you still greet someone even if you had a fight the day before.

> * Politeness in contrast is 'nice to have', but not necessary. It is an optional extra, a personal touch and is subject to much more individual variation than *Anstand*. It involves people being nice and friendly, e.g. a sales assistant giving advice.

An interesting example they gave to contrast *Anstand* and politeness was that *Anstand* is when an elderly person drops something and a younger person picks it up. Politeness is when a younger person drops something on the floor and an elderly person picks it up.

When I checked with the students whether I had portrayed their 'composite' definition accurately, some found it just right. One student commented that he personally would adjust the group definition a bit by describing politeness as 'desirable' and even 'normal' rather than just 'nice to have' or 'optional'. This illustrates the individual variation mentioned, that some people find politeness more important than others. However, the fact remains that politeness is a personal code, unlike *Anstand*, which is a basic code of behaviour that you can expect of others.

Keep your 'tie' on

Dr. Torsten Reimer, a German psychologist at Basel University, explains that in Germany the word *Anstand* is most often used for the behaviour of children. He gives as an example the expression 'Be good now', which in German would be *Sei anständig*. However, he points out that in Germany almost nobody would use the word nowadays. In Switzerland *Anstand* is alive and well, as the students' definitions show. Perhaps a suitable translation of the word in the Swiss context would be 'correct behaviour'. As typical examples mentioned by the students that day, it is correct behaviour to greet people, to wish them a nice meal when you start to eat and to say 'cheers' before you start to drink your wine or beer.

English speakers often underestimate these formalities, seeing them as an optional extra. Topics related to *Anstand* are repeated many times in this book, because their importance tends to be underestimated by English speakers. In the English-speaking world it shows you are relaxed and comfortable with people if you drop formalities. You can just walk into a room and say a general 'Hi' to the whole group. In German-speaking Switzerland you tend more to shake hands with everyone in the group and greet them all individually by name (using first names or surnames appropriately according to your relationship). German Swiss teenagers sometimes shake hands, and if they want to be cool, may slap each others' hands instead of shaking them. They still perform a ritual by which they greet others.

To help Swiss people understand why anyone would want to stop adhering to a ritual like greeting people correctly, I say it is a bit like Swiss men not wearing their tie at work if they don't have a client visit that day. They want to feel less formal and relax a bit.

> Ariane on shaking hands: In the French part of the country, customs are different. In the Geneva region, kids are taught to say *Bonjour*, too, but they don't really shake hands with adults. Recently, I visited a colleague from the circus school and met her three sons (5, 8 and 11) for the first time. They all spontaneously gave me three kisses on the cheek. The husband, who is German Swiss, shook hands with me when he arrived a little bit later, but we kissed each other on the cheek when I left.
>
> My nieces always said *tu* with first names to their kindergarten and primary school teachers, and never shook their hands. I wouldn't say that shaking hands among teenagers is really a common practice here.

Anstand would sound more appealing to English speakers if it was called 'appropriate' behaviour rather than 'correct' behaviour.

Describing it as 'correct' suggests it is a moral absolute with an authority behind it, and there is no such category in English for any code of behaviour other than the law. *Anstand* may not be a law, but it is a fundamental code agreed on and adhered to by a particular cultural group and as such has to be taken seriously. The formalities matter. It may be easier for Asians to grasp the importance of formalities than for westerners from more individualist countries. On the topic of politeness and face-saving, the Chinese sociolinguist L.R. Mao[12] comments:

> Chinese 'face' emphasises not the accommodation of individual 'wants' and 'desires', but the harmony of individual conduct with the views and judgment of the community.

In a pharmaceutical company, I overheard two office assistants discussing an American colleague who normally came into work in the morning and just walked to his desk without saying a word to them. They found this quite offensive, and one assistant was now training him by saying 'Good morning!' quite loudly and clearly every morning as he walked past.

It is not only English speakers who underestimate the importance of greeting people. Christine is German and has been reminded of this more than once:

'The first time I went to the Post Office I said *'Drei Briefmarken bitte'* (three stamps please). The assistant replied by saying *Grüezi*, to remind me that I had forgotten to greet her'.

Chapter 5 Dancing on the phone[13]

What does *Anstand* sound like on the phone? Catherine is Canadian and points out that when telephoning in the German speaking part of Switzerland, it is important to use greetings and use the other person's name correctly. If no one teaches you how to do it, it can take about three years to develop basic German Swiss telephone competence and another three to be truly sophisticated on the phone. You might like to speed up the process a little by studying the dialogues below. They are shown here in English (with a few German words for flavour) but it would be worth learning to do it in German.

You phone the travel agent (TA). Foremost on your mind is your upcoming flight to Canada. You begin with this when the travel agent picks up the phone.

Beginners level *(you handle it as you would in English)*

TA: Reisebüro Travel Corner, Keller.

You: I'd like to book a flight to Canada.

TA: Grüezi. What's your name please?

You have two left feet in the telephoning dance.

Intermediate level *(basic competence)*

TA: Reisebüro Travel Corner, Keller.

You: Grüezi. My name is Catherine Shultis. I'd like to book a flight to Canada.' (and while you are saying 'I'd like to book a flight to Canada', you are drowning out the travel agent, who is saying, 'Grüezi Frau Shultis').

You're still a bit out of step in the dance. You didn't say his name, or give him time to greet you.

Advanced level *(sophisticated phone user)*

TA   Reisebüro Travel Corner, Keller.

You: Grüezi Herr Keller. This is Shultis. (then you wait)

TA: Grüezi Frau Shultis

You: I'd like to book a flight to Canada

TA. Right....

At last you are dancing in step. The steps are as follows:

1. He gives his name
2. You greet him by name
3. You give your name
4. He greets you by name, and then
5. You tell him what you want

It is not a great crime if you do step five before he gets the chance to do step four, but many English speakers report that just when they are patting themselves on the back for having finally mastered it, they trip up again.

The dancing lesson could go on with reference to finishing the conversation using names again and possibly wishing each other a nice day, evening, weekend, or Sunday. In German if someone wishes you a nice something, you can reply *Danke, gleichfalls* (thanks, same to you).

Other telephone tips:

If you are phoning Heinz, and his wife, Sonja, answers the phone, tell her who's calling and have a few words with her too. Don't hang up when she says A*dieu, Tschüss* or 'Bye'. She is just going to get Heinz for you. Saying goodbye to you is a dance step too.

Sonja may come back and say, *Sind Sie noch da?* ('Are you still there?') Resist the temptation to reply 'No'. She doesn't really think you've gone away, it's just the Swiss way to make contact again, the way English speakers say 'hello' when they come back to the phone. In French they say *Ne quittez pas*. ('Don't go away') the way English and German speakers say 'Just a moment, please'.

Clearly labelled

One of the key issues in the telephone dance is giving your name to label yourself clearly. Many German Swiss find it strange if people are willing to get into discussion without knowing who they are talking to. Some even say their name to the operator at Directory Enquiries. They know she does not need this in order to give them a telephone number, but they feel they are treating her more respectfully if they use her name (which she gives when she answers the phone) and take the time to give her theirs.

In Switzerland it is important to have everyone clearly labelled, and people expect to know who they are dealing with. People who are not looking for clients are still invited to give their profession in the phone book, although this is becoming less common. When women get married, they will either keep their maiden name or attach it to the end of their married name so that people will always know who they are / were. (It makes phone books longer and name plates on letter boxes more expensive.)

People can also be 'placed' by their educational background. If you are the Head of Sales in a company, people would probably still like to know what kind of apprenticeship you completed before you moved into Sales. It is part of my label that I was an English teacher before I branched out into intercultural communication. There is a saying, *Ohne Herkunft keine Zukunft*, which means 'without origins, no future'.

Chapter 6 The language of the heart

Many Swiss people speak two or three languages, but English is not necessarily the one they are best at. Ken is a Scottish marketing manager who came to Switzerland assuming the Swiss would be really fluent in English and enjoy using it. He was then surprised at how little English the general population could speak.

> I imagined the Swiss to be more like the Dutch and the Scandinavians, throwing around English phrases in their everyday conversations, even if it was just a few expletives and a few MTV clichés, like 'cool man'. I did not find this to be the case.

British people often associate Switzerland with more northern European countries like the Netherlands, Germany and Scandinavia. In these countries school pupils usually learn English as a first foreign language, for five to nine years. Switzerland is different because of the four national languages which have to be juggled, as explained below.

In Switzerland it is assumed that everyone should be able to speak at least two of the national languages. In 60% of the cantons pupils learn a national language as their second language, and then

Ariane on Swiss languages: Switzerland is known and praised for its cultural diversity. Four different linguistic communities live together on a territory of 40,000 square km (around 15,000 square miles). Swiss German is mainly spoken in the northern and the eastern parts of the country, French in the western regions, whereas Italian is spoken in the south. The Romansch language can be heard mainly in two valleys in the heart of Switzerland.[14] Most books on Switzerland refer to the strong influence from France for the French-speaking Swiss, and some influence from Italy for the smaller Italian-speaking Ticino to explain the differences prevailing in these two minority regions, in comparison to the greater German-speaking part of Switzerland. The influence of neighbouring countries on the respective language communities is undeniable: as a French Swiss, you will follow the presidential election in France more eagerly than the one for the Chancellor in Germany. And you'll appreciate wine more than beer. But at the same time, the language communities distinguish themselves from their neighbouring countries of the same language family in some fundamental values. For example, the French are predominantly Catholic, whereas a number of Swiss French cantons are mainly Protestant (many Huguenots fled France in the 16th century and moved to Switzerland).

English as the third language, and in 30% of cantons they have the choice of Italian or English as their third language.[15] (60% of the citizens of the European Union speak either German, French or Italian, so these languages are also useful for travel and international business within Europe.)[16]

Some people may not have learnt English at all. It is often a matter of luck whether you deal with people who can speak it as you go shopping or have your washing machine repaired. Even students starting courses at Swiss universities may have only had five or six years of English, and are not necessarily offered English as part of their university curriculum. Heather Murray, university lecturer in English for Academic Purposes, reports in an article that at Berne University there are only three English courses per semester (each with 24 students) offering six lessons per week for the whole university. These courses cannot cover the needs of even 5% of students studying natural sciences.[17] It is astounding that given figures like this, there are so many Swiss scientists in industry speaking excellent English. They have often learnt it on their own in evening classes or during a stay abroad. (See also chapter 15 on English at work.)

If you think you are going to stay a while in Switzerland, it is worth learning the language of the region you are living in. The French Swiss have a different accent from the French, and they say themselves that they do not speak as 'eloquently' as the French, but this makes it easier for foreigners to learn the language. In the Italian-speaking part of the country an Italian dialect is also spoken, but not in the public domain, and like the French Swiss, Italian Swiss say they are not as eloquent as the Italians.

In the German-speaking part there is what linguists call diglossia, meaning that people read and write High German (standard German) but speak a dialect of Swiss German. If you learn High German you will be able to read notices, fill in forms, watch German films and start reading the newspaper. People will usually talk to you in High German if they hear you are a foreigner. If you learn Swiss German, you will more quickly understand German Swiss

TV and radio programmes and what German Swiss are saying to each other. It is rarely written. Most people recommend starting with High German and if you are in the country long enough, you will start to understand the local version of Swiss German automatically.

Dialect versus accent

Dialect is a complex matter, but a simplified definition could be as follows:

If a group of people are having a conversation and each person is using different words and grammar to talk about the same thing, they are probably speaking different dialects. For example in different Swiss-German dialects, going shopping can be called *einkaufen, posten* or *Kommissionen machen.*

If they are using the same words but pronounce the words a bit differently, they have different accents. If a group of Swiss and Germans read exactly the same sentence aloud in High German, you can hear immediately which ones have a Swiss accent and possibly where in Switzerland they come from.

A task approach to language classes

Try to find language classes which help you with the language for everyday situations. In my late teens I worked in Belgium with a Swiss boss, and English, Dutch and Swedish co-workers. It was my job to buy the bread for the lunch, and Elenor, my Swedish co-worker, taught me how to ask for it in Dutch (or Flemish[18]) at the bakery. So I waited in the bakery queue, and when it was my turn, said *'een groot bruin brood gesneden'* with a Swedish accent, and like magic, a large brown sliced loaf suddenly appeared in front of me. It was my first experience of using a language communicatively to get results, as my French and German classes at school had consisted mainly of grammar exercises and translation. I was pleased that it 'worked' and moved on to the next step of learning to count from 1-100 so that I could understand people telling me prices.

Good language lessons should teach you the basic structures of the language, but also identify the tasks you want to carry out in daily life and give you practice doing them in class. Try to get a recommendation as to a flexible teacher. If you have one-to-one lessons and know you will soon need to order heating oil or wood for your fireplace, or ask at the bakery if they sell milk, you should be able to practise a dialogue with the teacher to accomplish these things. It gives you a feeling of success in the language if you 'say your sentences' and things start to happen. Before you start one-to-one language classes, it is a good idea to ask if the programme can be tailored to your needs. If you join a group class this is not so easy to arrange.

Something else you might like to consider is asking your teacher to tell you a few of the local expressions. If the shop assistant asks whether you want a bag for your purchase, which dialect word does she use? (In Basel the word is *Gugge*, so it may sound as if people are offering you a coke or a cookie). Course books will teach you to say *Auf Wiedersehen* for 'goodbye' but the people around you might be saying *Adieu*, or something else.

Everyone learning German in Switzerland complains at some point that people speak the wrong language to them. If you are trying to learn High German it will seem as if everyone addresses you in Swiss German and if you are trying to learn Swiss German it will seem that everyone insists on speaking High German to you the moment they hear your foreign accent. People cannot always know which one you want, so you may have to ask them to change. Another problem may be that people insist on speaking English to you so that they can get some practice. You can insist on sticking to German. You are living in the country, and you need the practice more.

Dialect and identity

Why is dialect so important? Steve Pawlett is Canadian and makes the following comment:

> I am struck by the similarities between Swiss and Canadians. Both live beside giant economies, both are polite to a fault, and both struggle to find a place for themselves in the world.

Dialect is the language of the heart. It helps reinforce local identity as nations look for their place in the world. This is particularly an issue for Switzerland as a small country. The various Swiss German dialects give people the opportunity to express their regional roots and allegiances, and at the same time distinguish their country from their larger German neighbour. (As a joke Germany is sometimes referred to as the 'big canton'). Before the first world war, Swiss German was on the decline, but the two world wars reversed this trend. Globalisation has recently further increased interest in reinforcing local identity around the world.

In contrast with the German-speaking part of the country, dialect is not used in Ticino to the same extent in the public sphere.

Another use for dialect is to level out educational differences. Swiss German does not have such complicated sentence structures as High German. Urs Späti, Human Resources manager at Ciba Speciality Chemicals sees dialect as a leveller:

> The Swiss have a well-preserved democratic dialect, a kind of insular secret language shared by all insiders. An uneducated person can understand what a professor is actually saying, although he may not be able to understand the significance of it.

Swiss people also tend to speak a simpler version of High German than Germans, although this depends on individual linguistic ability. Children start learning High German at the age of six or seven in school and although they learn it pretty fast, most never quite catch up with the head start of children in Germany. German parents also read story books in High German to their pre-school children, which can give the children exposure to more complex sentences structures than they use with the child in the spoken language. Swiss parents tend to read a story in High German for themselves and then tell it in dialect in their own words. Germans are known for having a larger vocabulary, using longer, more complex sentences and having a more confident manner as they speak. According to a study by psychoanalyst Paul Parin reported in the 1970s, this can give German Swiss the impression that Germans are more intelligent, and Germans in turn can underestimate the intellectual capacity of the Swiss.[19]

It is true that Swiss German dialect often uses simple language to express complex truths but this does not mean that the dialects are underdeveloped. They have just as complex a grammar as any official language. I had been speaking Swiss German for about five years before I started to notice the subjunctives. You can say 'er isch' for 'he is' but if you say 'she says he is' you have to use 'er sig' instead of 'er isch' for 'he is' to remind people that it is reported speech and you are only quoting someone. Words like 'have' and 'go' all have their own subjunctive, (and of course each dialect has its variant forms too).

Andrea is German and a teacher of German to 10-13 year olds in Switzerland and finds there is a desire among parents for their children to speak better German than the parents themselves do.

Parents are happy that their children are learning German from a German. But dialect is very important to them at the same time. It is an interesting mix. Sometimes educated people apologise for their bad German when they talk to a German, but actually their German is good.

It would seem that more and more Swiss parents want their children to keep their dialects, but also to speak High German more eloquently. TV is helping in this regard. Educators sometimes jokingly call High German 'TV German' nowadays, because when children are role playing German TV programmes in the school playground, they do it in High German. It is quite a recent development that Swiss children are watching a lot of children's TV, and there are some high quality programmes (e.g. on the German *Kinderkanal*) which can help them improve their High German.

German for foreign children

It is important to understand the 'language plus dialect' situation if you are sending your children to German Swiss school. The teacher may speak High German to the class, but in primary school Swiss children will often speak Swiss German back and will certainly speak Swiss German in the playground. There is a tendency for people to underestimate the difference between the two variants of German, describing Swiss German as not being a 'fully developed language'. Even if this were true, it would not make it easier to learn.

Linguistically speaking, the difference between High German and Swiss German can be as great as the difference between High German and Dutch, depending on which Swiss dialect you use for comparison. It was for political reasons that the dialect of Amsterdam became the official standard of the Netherlands in the 17th century, and the Swiss decided to use High German as their standard rather than have to appoint one of their dialects to become the standard, and reduce the others to lower status. After all, 'the Queen's English', otherwise known as Received Pronunciation or BBC English, was once merely the dialect of the 'East Midlands', the region around London, Oxford and Cambridge.[20]

Some German Swiss schools start foreign children in special classes to get them used to the language first before transferring them to regular classes. Other schools offer a few weeks of High

German lessons with a private teacher before the children start Swiss school. The more fluent they are in High German when they start, the easier it will be for them to understand Swiss German too.

> In German Swiss kindergartens, the teacher and the children usually speak Swiss German together. If you are already living in Switzerland and want to send your child to Swiss school, it will be a great help if they can first learn the dialect at kindergarten. Then they will be in the same situation as the Swiss children, using their knowledge of Swiss German to help them learn to read and write and speak High German (as a quasi-foreign language) when they start school.

Dutch, German and Swiss German are all Germanic languages / dialects and are closely related, and it is easier to pick up one if you know another. The example (see below) shows how you say 'I don't have time' in the three languages, compared with English. There are regularities, such as the tendency in Swiss German to drop the 'n' endings of High German, as in *keine* changing to *kei*. Changing an 'i' sound (as in *Zeit*) to an 'ee' (as in *Ziit*) is also typical.

English:	I	have	no	time
Dutch:	Ik	heb	geen	tijd (*tide*)
German:	Ich	habe	keine	Zeit (*tsite*)
Swiss German:	I	ha	kei	Ziit (*tseet*)

Section two: Settling in locally

Chapter 7   Good fences make good neighbours

Varieties of experience

Tanya is from the USA and has lived in Basel for many years with her Swiss husband and two sons. She describes the contrasting experiences she has had in the different neighbourhoods she has lived in:

> First we lived in an apartment surrounded by mostly older neighbours, and we had very little contact, except when they had a complaint. In our second apartment the neighbours were also older, but this time we took the initiative to invite them over, like for an apero (a drink) after our baby's birth, and got to know them better. Then we moved to an apartment in a free-standing house on the edge of town, where houses were quite far apart and neighbours just said hello as they passed and seemed a bit shy at first. It took a while to get to know them, because we didn't run into each other so often.
>
> Finally, we moved into a townhouse on the other end of the first street we had lived on ten years before. By this time a lot of young families had moved in alongside the older people (it was about half / half) and we were surprised at how outgoing and

friendly they were. People came up to us and said. 'We're glad you've moved in!' and the first time my husband went out to do a bit of gardening, at least five people stopped to talk to him. Some invited us over for drinks. Several neighbours let me know that there were some lovely activities for young children at the local church, as well as annual family events such as meeting *Santiglaus* (Saint Nicolas, or Santa Claus) and a movie night at the local park. Many of the neighbours put up their Christmas lights on the same day and made a 'happening' out of it. Groups of children have even started spontaneous trick-or-treating on Halloween.

Our neighbours appear to be open to old and new traditions, but most importantly, they are interested in positive contact with each other. In general, I would say 'new' people take more initiative to make contact than older residents. It is like an American neighbourhood.

This example shows how difficult it is to generalise about what your relationships in a neighbourhood could be like, even within the same Swiss town. It is not only a question of how friendly you are, as Tanya knew. She mentions age and the influx of new people moving into the street as factors affecting how much contact people make. Another contributory factor could be that the friendliest neighbours all lived in town houses (or terraced houses), close enough to each other to make contact easily but with their own front doors so that they did not literally live on top of each other as they would have done in an apartment.

Should you expect respectful distance or a warm welcome when you move into a new neighbourhood? You cannot influence the 'neighbourhood culture' much, but you can create the best conditions to get off to a good start with others in it. Usually in the US the neighbours welcome *you* when you move in. In Switzerland many people say it is up to you as the newcomer to make the first move and introduce yourself when you move in. Tanya's experience was different, as people approached her, and Jeanne and Chip, an American couple, reported to me that their neighbours organised an apero (drinks party) to welcome them to their new neighbourhood. However, because of the high value placed on independence, people are just as likely to respect your privacy and wait for you to signal that you want contact. It could be seen as nosey for existing neighbours to go up to the newcomer's door as they're just moving in, as if they want to get a look at their furniture.

> Janice, who is from the USA, said she took a small gift to a family as they were moving in, to say hello and introduce her own family. The woman was quite taken-aback, and said, 'but we're not settled in yet!' People may not want you to see their mess and prefer to be left alone as they get settled. When we moved into a new apartment our neighbour left a lovely plant arrangement on our doormat to welcome us. It was then up to us to ring her bell when we were ready to make contact.

Little rituals

If you want to get to know your neighbours, it is important to be properly introduced, so that people know who you are. You can then greet your neighbours by name in the German-speaking part of the country. In the French and Italian parts you just say *Bonjour Monsieur / Madame* and *Buon Giorno Signor / Signora* respectively, when you pass in the street. Some newcomers ring the neighbours' bell, others wait until there is a chance encounter on the stairs or in the garden. As mentioned by Tanya, it is common in urban areas for younger people to invite the neighbours round to an Open House or apero and this often leads to good contacts, especially among people who potentially have something in common (for more details see chapter 10 on entertaining). Aperos are appreciated in some neighbourhoods more than others. In more traditional or country communities they will not necessarily be understood, as Max, a Swiss manager from the region of Lucerne reports. He and his family recently came back from 15 years living and working in Thailand and had what he describes as a disastrous cocktail party.

We were used to the expatriate scene in Thailand, where cocktail parties are held regularly to introduce new arrivals. These were very international affairs, with people from many different countries. When we moved into a village on the Lake of Lucerne we had a similar kind of cocktail party. We called it 'open house' and made a nice invitation for all the neighbours. It was a disaster. It just isn't done in the Lucerne area. You only invite people you know. Some came to look at the house, sniffed around, then left after 20 minutes. With others you could see they found it strange. 'What do these people want? Why are they inviting us for wine and snacks? Why would I want to socialise with this neighbour or that one?' It also didn't work to have more small-scale dinners and barbecues for people who didn't know each other. They didn't know what to talk about. Native English-speakers are much better at making small talk with complete strangers. They can keep it up for a whole evening. In the end we got to know some of the neighbours more easily through their kids, who came to play regularly with our kids. This was more effective than the cocktail party.

Peach and coconut sub-cultures can both be found in Switzerland, where some people will invite people they hardly know into their homes and others wouldn't feel comfortable about it. In Tanya's new neighbourhood, her family were invited for drinks or coffee by various people. In Max's neighbourhood, people were quite reserved, and breaking the ice by inviting people to the house was too big a step. As he describes, contact is often more easily made through the children, and the value of chatting to people one-to-one in their gardens, at the shops or on the staircase of the apartment block or walking your dog should also not be underestimated. People sometimes stop for a brief chat and then, as they get to know each other, it can easily turn into an hour spent in the hallway between the apartments.

Having a coffee or a meal together tends to be a more formal event, especially for the older generation, and is usually preceded by an invitation. The younger generation may invite each other in for a coffee more spontaneously. Swiss people who have lived abroad themselves may also have a more laid-back approach, and some people just enjoy getting to know others from around the world. It depends a lot on the individuals you happen to meet.

What is neighbourliness?

Your definition of 'neighbourliness' may depend on where you have come from. Sam and June moved from the north of England to Switzerland, to a free-standing house in a small village. After they had been there a week, they had a crisis on their hands. June tells the story.

We found the cellar flooded, from melted snow coming in the window. We had no idea why it was happening, and we hadn't a clue what to do. Sam had once had a friendly chat with a man across the road who spoke English, so he went to ask for his help. He wasn't any help at all. He came as far as the front door, said, 'It sounds like you've got a problem', and left again. Sam then went to a very nice older neighbour and in pidgin French, got him to understand the problem and then the neighbour phoned the fire brigade for him. However, we were surprised that he didn't come to the house to take a look until after it was all over. The Fire Brigade came and sorted out the problem, and we were left puzzling over the differences between our neighbours in England and Switzerland.

Sam and June had just left a particularly friendly neighbourhood in the north of England where everyone regularly popped in and out of each others' houses. In a case of flooding, neighbours would have provided moral support, coming into the house to have a look and showing an interest in the problem, and if possible, helping solve it. In Switzerland this could be seen as nosey and intrusive if the people were not good friends. The older man helped them, but was no doubt respecting their privacy by not coming in to see the mess. Maybe the neighbour who spoke English assumed they were inviting him to roll up his sleeves and start baling, and he didn't want to get involved (see box: That's not your job). If he was cautious by nature, he might have been thinking, 'If I do this for them now, where will it end?'

Although neighbours respect each others' privacy, it is typical that they go into each others' houses by arrangement, e.g. to organise looking after plants or pets for each other when they go on holiday, and they may do this very conscientiously. One year when we were on holiday and our neighbours were looking after our plants, they were woken at 2 am by a storm and very heavy rain. They knew our balcony drain tended to get blocked and so the husband went over in his pyjamas to bale out the water. It certainly wasn't his job, or part of the arrangement with us but we appreciated his concern.

That's not your job
Dianne tells the story of her Swiss friends, Martha and Hans (manager of a Swiss firm) who went to visit her sister in Florida.

Hans couldn't believe it when he saw my sister's neighbour, a surgeon, on a Sunday afternoon under his car, leisurely changing the oil. Hans thought a surgeon shouldn't get his hands dirty doing menial work like that since he could easily afford to hire someone for such dirty work. Besides, in Switzerland most repair jobs are done by people who have learned these crafts, and are experts with a certificate to prove it. For safety reasons it is against the law to do electrical jobs in the home yourself, e.g. put up light fittings. My sister (who had hoped Hans would have a look at a problem on her roof) thought Hans' reaction showed that he must either be lazy, a snob or have two left hands.

Pioneer traditions

Jane is American and comments that the US was originally populated by people who had left their support networks in another country and were pioneers, starting a new life in what was originally a wilderness. They were often dependent on the kindness of strangers, and there were no organised institutions to call upon. This was then the foundation for neighbourliness in the sense of an exchange of practical help. (It is difficult to translate the word 'neighbourliness' into other languages and keep the English meaning). Nowadays, with people in the USA moving house about once every five years, these relationships can be of short duration, and people tend not to feel they are getting into something 'for life'.

The importance of boundaries

All cultures need boundaries of some kind as people mark their territory, as illustrated in Robert Frost's poem, 'Mending wall', about two neighbours who keep remaking the wall that marks the division of their land. One is more keen to build the walls ('Good fences make good neighbours') and the other has a reluctance to create walls and questions those which exist ('Something there is which doesn't love a wall, which wants it down').

Switzerland is a landlocked country surrounded by foreign land rather than open sea. Many communities also have natural boundaries created by mountains and valleys. In the past these have protected them against enemies.

Within the community, the boundaries may be physical or psychological. If people live in houses, their 'good fences' may be in the physical garden fence, and in an apartment block, their front doors.

People often live very close to the same neighbours for most of their lives and some feel they need psychological distance to offset the physical closeness. Although the psychological walls or fences are there, they can be removed if people want them down. Some people may assume that once you start getting involved with others, it may be difficult to back out again. In Switzerland some neighbours do get to know each other well, helping and supporting each other, especially when they have young families, but you cannot assume that everyone is comfortable doing this.

A preference for self-reliance

Traditionally in Swiss culture, people try to be self-reliant and not disturb others. (A mother jokingly told me she would rather lay an egg herself than disturb others by asking for one.) Neighbours will also not like to threaten a newcomer's independence by offering advice or help which has not been asked for, as if the newcomer 'can't manage'. The new person often has to signal that they would like advice or help. It may be a matter of getting to know your neighbour a bit first, to get a feeling for the give and take in your relationship (although asking for information should never be a problem).

Younger people are more likely to help each other out, and I have heard of new housing developments where people lend out tables for parties, or offer the use of their ovens and dishes. Christine, who is Swiss, points out that as people get older, and less mobile, they are also more willing to be dependent on others, preferably of their own generation. Where it is one-sided, people are careful to owe nothing (see below).

Build your wine collection
Olivia told the story of lending her corkscrew to her younger neighbour who was having a party. It was good for opening particularly wide-necked bottles. He returned it the next day with a bottle of wine as thanks.

Heinz then said he once carried down the old paper for the rubbish collection for an elderly neighbour and bought something for her at the mobile shop outside the door. She rewarded him with an excellent bottle of wine.

The helpers were happy to do so and did not necessarily expect to be so well rewarded. The fact that they were is more a sign of the obligation felt by the person asking for the favour.

In English, when people ask for help, they use expressions like, 'Sorry to trouble you but . . .' or 'Do you think you could possibly . . . ?' I used to find French Swiss and particularly German Swiss students quite resistant to these polite expressions when I was teaching them English. They could not see any use for them. 'If you're ever in trouble you will need them', I assured them. Now I am not so sure.

People in Switzerland are well-organised to be self-reliant, and practical help is mainly provided by the family and close friends. They are committed to helping their in-group and there is no need for persuasive language. They will also more readily call in professionals for help than in countries with a strong 'do-it-yourself' tradition, as the flood emergency showed.

As well as cultivating relationships with your neighbours, it may also help to meet newcomers or Swiss people from other regions who are new to the area and interested in getting to know others quickly. In our early days as parents with a young baby in Switzerland, my husband and I had no family nearby, and there were no young families in the neighbourhood. My support group, or 'substitute family' consisted of other foreign mothers of various nationalities. We were all in the same boat and were committed to helping each other out, for example when one of us was ill and needed help with the children. In this way my husband and I did not need to impose on our neighbours who had no children, and many of whom were out at work all day.

A ritual breaking down of barriers

In some parts of the country there are special occasions in which people go into each others' houses. Mary is Scottish and has lived 20 years in a quiet street in a small village in Ticino, the Italian part of Switzerland. She is on first name terms with many people in the village, in particular with the parents of her children's friends, but not with the neighbours in the other houses on her small private road. They all pass by and greet each other, saying politely, *Buon giorno Signor / Signora* but they do not stop to talk. Something has to happen before they will disturb each other's privacy, as Mary describes:

> Our youngest daughter Linda died tragically at the age of 12 when she was out cycling. It was three days before I was able to see her, because of the required post mortem examination. When they finally released Linda's body, I wanted to have it at home. A friend warned me that our house would be full of people if I did this, which I just could not imagine, given the way people normally kept their distance. However it was a Catholic village, and it turned out to be the case that I had given the signal for people to come. There was a steady stream of people for three days, coming to pay their respects, including many older people.

By having the body brought home, Mary had made it clear to her neighbours that she was inviting the community to come and mourn with her and her family. As a result of this she now had increased contact with many people she had known only from a distance before. It should be mentioned here that in the German-speaking part of Switzerland people rarely have the body at home but may have a service in a chapel before burial, where the body is in a closed casket.

Boundaries within the home

Even when people are invited into each other's houses, different cultures view the boundaries within the home differently.

What is 'public' and what is 'private'? If you are invited for dinner, should you 'pitch in' by fetching things from the kitchen, or even the fridge? Probably not. I remember being very surprised when a group of Tamil women visited my home in Switzerland. After a cup of tea they all marched into the kitchen with their cups, and each one washed her own. It was a gesture of thoughtfulness to save me the work. As a guest in Switzerland, you are usually not expected to go into the kitchen (unless that's the room you're eating in). If you ask guests to help themselves to a second helping of food from the buffet you've set up in the kitchen, you may find no one moves and you have to bring the food to them instead. They are respecting the boundaries of your private sphere.

Another room which can be part of your public or private sphere is the bedroom. In Scotland, if people have a lot of visitors, they may put all the coats on the bed, and then the visitors go and fish their coats out of the pile when they are going home. In Switzerland I did this too in the early days, and a Swiss visitor once said our apartment looked great, and all that was missing was a coat stand in the hall. He probably didn't feel comfortable fetching his jacket from the bedroom.

Chapter 8   Join the club

(or the *Verein, Assoziazione*, or *Association*)

For highly mobile people, offering and receiving practical support is a survival strategy but can also be a way of getting to know people and maintaining contact in the neighbourhood. In this way they can create community wherever they go. It makes sense if you have no close friends or family around. Swiss people tend to have their needs for support met within their 'insider' group, and they signal the desire to get more involved with people in a more clear-cut way, almost officially, by joining a sports club, exercise class, a local church, political group or women's organisation. In his book on the Basel Fasnacht, the carnival, Peter Habicht comments 'We Swiss do love a club to organise and structure our hobbies'.[21]

Max is Swiss, from a village near Lucerne and recommends two steps to get to know the locals.

> First, make every effort to learn the language. It requires a big effort, but it opens so many doors and is much appreciated by local people. Then it is easier to join local clubs, like the sports or gymnastics clubs you find in nearly every town and village for different age groups. A lot of people in these clubs can't speak English. If you can speak their language, they will think 'this person's

not bad' and are more likely to invite you to take part in their other activities which are also going on outside the club, e.g. at the weekend.

Swiss people who move into a new neighbourhood may also join clubs to make contact. When my children were small, I joined a local women's group. The other members were all Swiss, but we discovered after many years that only one of the 12 women actually came from the town we lived in. The others were from other towns, but had married local men. By joining the structured group they were able to develop closer relationships over a period of years.

Members of a club may see each other more often than they do their long-standing friends, and they use first names there as they do with friends. The meaning of club rituals should not be underestimated, as Val, from England, describes.

> There are rituals that still hit me every time I turn up for the exercises at the local ski club. There are 60 people present, and everyone shakes hands with everyone else, and greets them by first names before we start running around in a circle. It's quite hard because you're meant to know all the names. The same thing happens at the canoeing club.

Although it can be hard to remember sixty names, it is a good sign if you have an in-group of people to be on first-name terms with. You may discover you 'belong' to a greater degree than you had expected. There can be a level of commitment involved in joining such a group. In many countries if you stop turning up regularly at a club, they just forget about you. In Switzerland you continue to belong if you stop going for a while because of other commitments, or if you can only make it occasionally. They understand being 'busy' but may have a long-term perspective of relationships. Another feature of groups is that some meet only every two weeks or once a month. This is also a long-term orientation, 'We have all our lives to spend together, there's no rush'. If you do leave, you may find people will still never forget you.

In contrast to the more traditional sports clubs, there are now fitness centres sprouting all over the country. These are competition for the traditional clubs and are not so useful to get to know people. You can come and go as you like, there is no sense of belonging, and you do not perform the symbolic handshake with anyone. The only purpose is exercise. In general, club activity is declining in urban Switzerland along with declining church attendance and a decline in active involvement in political parties.[22] Individualism is increasing. In rural areas, however, club activity still plays a central role in bringing people together and as Deborah, from the USA, points out, it is also a leveller, cutting across social classes.

Mary reports on a type of club which makes it possible for everyone in her Ticino village to belong somewhere:

> I grew up in Scotland, but because I was born in 1947 I automatically get an invitation to the annual class reunion of the local village primary school class of my age group. All classes organise these. The members pay a yearly subscription fee, and put an announcement in the paper every year, like 'The people born in 1947 are organising a dinner'. Attending these events automatically

gets you in with your own age group, from all walks of life. The majority of the original year group still live in the same village.

This is a very inclusive village custom which makes an effort to integrate outsiders by giving everyone a year group to belong to. The 'newcomers' can easily be integrated into the existing classes, without threatening the identity of the group.

In Switzerland a lot is done to encourage people to get involved in clubs. Val is English and is impressed by the work done by leaders of her son's ski club:

> I'm still totally bowled over by the enthusiasm and dedication of the young men and women who put a tremendous amount of time and energy into taking other peoples' kids skiing, training them, driving a minibus up and down the country, all for free. These trainers are all people in their early 20s, without even the impetus of having their own offspring in the same group. The junior subscription of Fr 40 a year can't even cover the petrol, so I guess that financially the club has to float on sponsorship and voluntary contributions from parents and well-wishers.

Chapter 9 Think local

If you work in an international environment in Switzerland, it may not immediately be obvious that your cosmopolitan Swiss colleagues live their private lives in clearly-defined small communities. Even though a Swiss husband may regularly be travelling to New York and Paris on business, his wife and family might have all their schooling, classes and clubs within a couple of kilometres of their house and walk or cycle everywhere. Even in larger towns with less close-knit communities than small villages, people may still operate within the immediate neighbourhood, breaking down the town into more manageable units.

We live in Riehen, a small town of 20,000 inhabitants. When we moved house from the south of Riehen, Riehen *Süd*, a few kilometres further north to Riehen *Dorf* (village), I continued to take my younger daughter to her playgroup in Riehen *Süd*. Although it was only 10 minutes by bike from north to south, people from 'the south' were surprised to see me at the supermarket there and commented that I was travelling far. I dismissed this idea, being of the opinion that these invisible boundaries were only in the mind.

However, when my daughter started kindergarten, I realised that she hardly knew any of the other neighbourhood children, while many of the others had already got to know each other at the play-group nearby, which was within walking distance. This was a practical consequence of the localised thinking.

In Switzerland most communities try to provide a kindergarten and school in the immediate neighbourhood so that children can walk there unaccompanied. Parents also prefer not to have to go far to take their children to their after-school classes. Ideally the children should walk or cycle there alone. Mothers who drive their children across the city to the best dancing class in the region are considered to be stressing their children and living a very stressful life themselves.

Given the very localised thinking, in what kind of a community are you likely to feel at home in Switzerland? When you are looking for a place to live, it is worth considering this in addition to checking out the amenities such as public transport, schooling or shops.

While many people still see the various language regions (French, Italian, German and Romansch speaking) as providing the starkest contrast, there is more and more an awareness of differences in mentality between urban and rural communities. This comes out clearly in the more conservative voting patterns of rural communities compared with those of urban areas. Cities are usually much more progressive in their attitudes, and the contrast with villages only a 20 minutes train ride away can be dramatic. This is not only experienced by foreigners, but also by mobile Swiss people settling in a new area.

Close-knit communities

The character of a village may be strongly influenced by geographical features. Does one village flow into the next, or is there
a mountain, hill or river providing a clear divide between them?
Isolated villages are usually more conservative. Vreni B. is Swiss
and grew up in such a village. She describes the significance of
outside influences for the local people in a close-knit community:

It used to be that every mountain village had a school so that
children didn't need to leave the village. This is no longer the case.
Every village has its own culture, and the people hope the children
will be satisfied with it and that it will be possible for them to continue to live in it. If schools are closed and children have to go
down to the town in the valley, they are exposed to outside influences and the local culture is watered down. These are not even
bad outside influences, but they make the mountain village look
narrow in comparison. It is also threatening to the survival of the
community when people go to the main city to work. Then they are
exposed to many new influences.

My parents live in a small Catholic village in Canton Solothurn. Recently a lot of newcomers moved in from Olten because
my parents' village is less foggy. The locals are Catholic, and very
conservative. For example, a girl who gets pregnant would have
to get married. The new people changed the political landscape,
introducing a more left-wing political party to the village, where
before there were only the more conservative parties. The newcomers turned everything upside down. But they were not rooted
there, and after four years they had all left again.

As well as geographical features, the attitudes of a village towards foreigners can be significant, as can the number of incomers who have paved the way for you. It is well worth asking other 'outsiders' (not necessarily foreigners) about their experiences, especially if you are planning to build or buy a house and settle in a community. This is particularly relevant if you are going to send your children to the local school. The fact that a village is only 20 minutes by train from the city does not mean it is progressive. It will have its own identity.

Jake Christ,[23] a Swiss psychiatrist who returned to Basel after having worked for 25 years in the USA, believes Americans can easily misjudge the importance of little communities:

> Swiss local communities have a great deal of political autonomy from the cantonal government and the federal government in Bern. They have tax money, some more, some less, AND political clout. They are not simply satellites of big cities, which is what most American suburbs are like. They have structures built in, both political and social. On the positive side, the clear sense of community characteristic of Switzerland was illustrated in a 'mental health in the community' project I started in Basel Land. In the States I had been involved in similar projects, but found them much easier to implement in Switzerland, because communities were so clearly defined. You knew exactly where one community ended and the next began. It was easy to know which organisation to ask to do what.

> Local communities may determine which foreign residents may become Swiss citizens. Some communities put it up to the voters to decide the qualifications of each person seeking citizenship. Others simply have rules that have to be followed. By con-

trast, in the USA, citizenship is determined by the federal government, not local government.

If you want to get involved in the life of a close knit community, wait a few months until you get a feel for what's going on and who's running what. It is typical that in highly mobile communities volunteers are constantly needed for clubs, churches, etc. to fill the gap left by people moving on. Your ideas for new clubs and groups may also be very welcome. In a more static community, people may all have their roles and some will be holding positions they have held for 20 or 30 years. If you have new ideas, it might help to test them on some insiders you get on well with, before you present them to the whole community. Swiss incomers from other villages may need to do this too.

Educational considerations

It may be that you will work in one canton and can choose to live in another. People working in Basel Stadt, for example often live in Basel Land and can still reach the city centre by tram in 20 minutes. Some move further out to other cantons, like Aargau or Solothurn where properties are less expensive. Newcomers usually look into the tax implications when choosing where to live. Cantonal school systems also differ, and it goes beyond the scope of this book to describe 26 different school systems, and, depending on the age of your child, different school cultures. As an example, in some cantons children are selected for the academic track at the age of 11, in others, this is done when they are 13. In some school systems, parents have the final word on whether their child takes the academic track while in others the decision will be made by the primary school teacher alone. This type of issue is not only decided by academic achievement, but also by the child's character and behaviour record. A child who gets good grades, but does not seem to be very mature may not be recommended for the academic track. If you are thinking of sending your child to a Swiss school, and you have a choice of where to live, it may be worth checking out the different school systems.

Chapter 10 Entertaining

The way people socialise and entertain can reflect their deep cultural values. Is socialising an opportunity to 'cast your net wide' and meet lots of new people or to deepen the relationships you already have? Do you want to talk to the same person for ten minutes or for three hours at a social gathering? People with a long-term approach to relationships will go more for the latter. This affects the way dinners, parties and other social gatherings are organised.

Different time scales

Ursula and Walter are Swiss and lived with their children in the USA for many years. Ursula commented on how the busy lifestyle of American parents influenced their entertaining customs:

> We were really surprised the first time we invited some people for a meal. After an hour and a half everyone was gone again. The food was finished but only the food, and for us that's not where it finishes. We interpreted their leaving early as meaning they didn't feel comfortable but later we understood that it was because of

their active lifestyle, picking up their daughter from sports, or driving their son to his piano lesson. In general the American parents we knew would rarely spend the whole evening eating with others.

In English-speaking cultures, if people are invited to an informal supper which starts in the early evening, they might expect it to be finished after 2 or 3 hours. In contrast, a more formal dinner party could last the whole evening. In Switzerland it is unusual to invite people for a meal which only lasts a couple of hours. Even if the invitation sounds informal, people will expect to spend the whole evening together. Walter commented that Swiss people would normally sit around the table and talk till midnight, finishing off the wine, or drinking coffee.

Younger Swiss people may also prefer to spend more time with fewer people on social occasions. Corinne is Swiss and travelled in Canada with a young group of English and Australian tourists. She joined them in the pub every evening after the day's tour.

'By Swiss standards it was like Fasnacht (the carnival). They were going from pub to pub, and just wanted to have a laugh together. They would just start talking to anyone. You had the feeling it didn't matter whether people were talking to you or someone else. In a Swiss tour group people would have split up and gone out in pairs or smaller groups in the evening, maybe for dinner. They would need to know each other longer before going for a drink as a group and would need a bit of a warming up time to become better acquainted with each other'.

In Switzerland there is often a preference for spending more time with fewer people. Lili is Ticinese, but grew up in Basel. She describes the intimacy of the Swiss way of entertaining people over a long dinner:

> In Switzerland you invite good friends, maybe two couples, and if the people you want to invite do not know each other, you check with them first if that will be okay. I enjoy meeting new people and getting to know them properly, with plenty of time to have long conversations over the course of a whole evening.

The party

The word party conjures up different images in different countries. If someone invites you to their birthday party in Switzerland, you will probably find yourself invited to a long sit-down meal. Sharon is from the USA and her husband Roger is Swiss. They decided to have a party for 20 friends in Basel just after they got married. She was amazed to see him prepare for it by filling the living room with large tables from the cellar. It was clear to her that if you wanted to have 20 people milling around your living room, you would first need to move some furniture out. For Roger it was clear that if you invited 20 people, you had to be able to seat them all at a table.

Mental images are hard to shift. When I am invited to a barbecue, I still always imagine people lazing around on deckchairs, with their plates on their laps, as is common in Britain. In Switzerland a buffet meal, indoors or outside, usually involves helping yourself to food at one table and then going to another table to sit down and eat it. When you serve yourself again, you usually go back to the same seat afterwards. Ursula comments:

> As a Swiss I feel it's rude to change places too early because it's like saying to your neighbour at the table 'you're not interesting enough'. The earliest time to change places is normally when coffee is served.

A critical incident

I had lived in Switzerland for a year when I arranged for one of my English classes, all German Swiss and French Alsatians, to come for a buffet meal after class. I expected them to pile the food up on their plates, sit around the room on the soft chairs with their plates on their laps, and get up to refill them from time to time. They might then change seats to get a chance to talk to different people. When they arrived, I gestured in the direction of the table and told them to take a plate. They all just stared at the table as if thinking 'What on earth does she want us to do?', so I handed a plate to Doris to get her started. She said, 'We need to make some space here' and started pushing the dishes of food into the middle of the table so that there was room to put her plate down. The others followed. They were very determined. They all pulled up chairs, got themselves plates and cutlery, set places for themselves and sat round the table. Then the serving could begin. I felt frustrated that I couldn't get them to do it my way, but at the back of my mind was the realisation that 'eating at tables' must have some deep cultural relevance worth exploring.

Stand-up events

Stand-up parties are often dreaded events in Switzerland (see also 'Small talk' in chapter 20). People like to eat and drink sitting at the table and tend not to like having to keep starting new conversations with different people. However, if you find yourself at a stand-up event and you are a good conversationalist with lots of ideas what to talk about, people may be pleased to talk to you. Ursula comments:

> We Swiss generally enjoy the difference of the more outgoing mentality of other countries. It is refreshing to us and we welcome it.

I recently attended an information day for non-Swiss on Swiss schools, presented by the American Women's Club of Basel, and was fascinated at how many new people I met in the course of a coffee break and a stand-up buffet lunch. Everyone was being introduced to new people by others and nobody minded that they often broke into each other's conversations. Interrupting seemed to be one of the rules of the game, and I had lots of stimulating little ten minute conversations with people. Obviously the fact that the group was homogenous with the topic of schooling in common made it easier to start chatting to anyone. The whole phenomenon reminded me of oil lamps with coloured blobs of oil, forming and re-forming at will. It was also clear that anyone who really wanted to chat in peace to the same person for half-an-hour would need to arrange to meet them again.

Shortly afterwards I attended an apero (or cocktail party) as a guest lecturer on the opening day of a university course. There I also spoke to many students, who were mostly Swiss, but the rules of the game were different. People were keen to meet their fellow students and wanted to talk to a variety of people, but as long as people were already talking to someone, others would hesitate to approach them. If discussion partners stood around silently, others would then feel free to join them. In some cases people stood at the edge of a discussion and waited until the discussion partners turned to them and involved them too. If you need to talk to someone in particular at such a gathering, rather than interrupt, you could stand near the person and try and catch their eye and when they turn to you, you start to speak. Dan, an American professor, reports that this approach is also normal behaviour at US parties related to academic events.

Practical tips

Dinner

Food: People may offer anything from a simple meal to an elaborate meal. As a basic meal you might have a salad, a main course and a light dessert, possibly with the salad as a starter. Younger people like to try new things, and will often be interested in foreign specialities.

Drinks: People generally offer dry white wine as an aperitif and either dry white or red wine with the meal. Mineral water is appreciated too, as it does not interfere with the taste of the wine. Apart from that, there is a wide range of soft drinks you could have on offer and nothing in particular is really typical. Tap water is not usually offered to guests.

Arriving for dinner

If you invite people to dinner for 8, they are likely to be there promptly, by 8.05 at the latest in German-speaking Switzerland. They might even come at 7.55. They will expect the same of you if they invite you. (If they are running more than 15 minutes late, they may call and say how late they will be). In Ticino 8.15 would also be okay but 8.30 is getting a bit late. If you say 'come between 7.30 and 8' some people will come at 7.30 on the dot and others will then come later. If you are used to having that extra 15 minutes to finish getting ready, try to imagine you told them to come at 7.15.

As the guests arrive, they will shake hands with everyone present and greet them by name. Relatives and good friends may also kiss each other lightly on the cheek.

Kissing people lightly on the cheek is a fairly new phenomenon in German-speaking Switzerland. It still varies as to whether
family members and friends shake hands or kiss each other when
they meet and say goodbye. When I came to Switzerland in 1987
my husband's brothers and sisters all kissed their mother and
shook hands with each other. Now some of them kiss each other
and others still shake hands. We began with two kisses in the early
90s and changed over to three in the mid- 90s, when, according to
Das Magazin, there seems to have been a standardisation process
going on.[24]

On informal visits, some Swiss people automatically take off
their shoes when they go into someone's house, and others ask
their hosts if they should. If you have a row of shoes near your
door, people will assume they should take theirs off too.

Wendy is English and remembers an incident when she first
came to visit me in Switzerland. We were sitting having lunch, and
suddenly my six-year-old daughter asked, 'Mummy, is Wendy
British?'. I said yes, and my daughter commented, 'I thought so.
She's still got her shoes on'.

Important rituals

In Switzerland certain little rituals are considered good manners and should not be omitted. Some of these points may also be
discussed elsewhere, but are listed together below for easy reference.

* Before starting to eat, say *bon appetit* or in Swiss-German, *en guete*. Usually you wait till the hostess is ready to eat before starting.

* Wait till the host or hostess (officially it is meant to be the host) says 'cheers' (*prost* or *santé*) before you start your wine. You can also say cheers with mineral water nowadays; it doesn't need to be alcohol.

* People hold the glass by the stem as it sounds better for clinking glasses. Everyone says cheers to the whole group and then clinks glasses with each other person at table and say cheers individually. It is becoming fashionable not to clink glasses at high class gatherings (see chapter 16 on business entertaining). Try to wait and let the others take the lead.

* It is important to look people in the eye as you say cheers, and in some cantons, especially towards the east of the country, it is also considered important to say the person's name (see box next page, Tell me my name).

* Swiss people often say 'thank you' for the invitation as they clink glasses or as they start to eat.

Tell me my name

When I first met my future husband's family in canton St Gallen we all introduced ourselves by our first names. When we sat down to dinner, the wine was poured and we raised our glasses I noticed everyone was saying *Prost* (cheers) and clinking with everyone else in the room, and so I copied them. My future brother-in-law, Martin, clinked glasses with me and said, '*Prost* Margaret'. '*Prost*', I replied. There was a pause, then he said, 'My name is Martin'. I know, I said, puzzled. 'You should say it when you clink glasses', he told me.

Gifts

It is difficult to generalise about gifts because this is personal and varies a fair bit. Some people will bring you flowers or a plant or some expensive chocolates even if they only drink one coffee and eat nothing. They are thanking you for opening up your home to them.

People coming for a meal might bring a bottle of wine, others bring wine and flowers. Some people think in terms of how many of them you are feeding and multiply the gift value by that amount. If you have children, they might bring something for the children. If they are invited to a birthday party, they will take a birthday present and the wine or flowers. It is meant to be good manners to unwrap the flowers before handing them to the host or hostess, but most people haven't read etiquette books and don't bother. In English-speaking cultures when people have been invited to dinner, they usually consider that they owe their hosts coffee or a meal in return. In Switzerland there is no automatic reciprocity, and people may express their thanks with generous presents rather than a return invitation. Many people try to avoid being stressed by too many social engagements. These should not be obligations.

The apero

An apero is really a term for a stand-up drinks party, where there will not be much to eat and you are not expected to stay long. Although the name 'aperitif' implies that it is before dinner, you may attend a cultural event at 7 pm and have an apero to follow at 8.30. It is becoming common for people to organise an apero when they move in to a new area and want to meet the neighbours. If you give a finishing time for your apero, e.g. 17.00-19.00, people will drop in at various times, but you can be sure your house will be cleared by 19.00. If you want to give people the option of staying longer, only mention the starting time, 'from 17.00'. If you provide plenty of chairs to sit on and tables for people to sit at, or at least put their drinks down on, they will be more comfortable and also more inclined to hang around. Some people will only stay half an hour if they have to stand. If you want them to stay longer, invite them for dinner. Then they might stay till 1 am.

Apero drinks: If you offer a choice of dry white wine, red wine, mineral water and orange juice, you can't go wrong. Add anything you personally like to this list. If you feel unsure about which wine to choose, make a note of the names of the various wines on special offer at the supermarkets in your price range and ask an 'expert' among your neighbours in advance which would be best. Be reassured that many people 'of means' offer ten-franc wines when they are entertaining large numbers. A wine-tasting apero organised as a competition can be a good ice-breaker as it gives people a task. Cover up the labels and get them guessing as to what kind of wine they are and which one is the best quality. Wine is a good conversation topic.

Apero food: If people will be standing, the best kind of snacks are finger foods which do not need a plate, but can be held with a serviette, eaten in a mouthful or two, and the serviette dumped. Keep in mind that people need to be able to shake hands. It is a nightmare for some Swiss people to hold a glass in one hand, a large unwieldy sandwich in the other, and then try and shake hands and remember the names of 20 new people as they arrive.

'Spot the foreigner'
If there are no tables available, English-speaking people often put things out of the way under their chairs. Most Swiss people do not do this (the risk of spillage is too great). I have observed this custom at events attended by local Swiss people and native English speakers from around the world. The guests are offered a drink when they arrive, and it is interesting to play 'spot the foreigner' as some people (including myself) pop their glasses under their chairs when the talk starts.

Coffee / tea events

If you are inviting a group of women, or just one person to your house, you could ask them for coffee rather than an apero. If you offer tea, you may find people ask for a herb or fruit tea, as these are just as popular as black tea. Instant coffee is fairly unpopular (and considered cheap). In general, coffee with a 'head' on it, made in the espresso machine (although not necessarily of true espresso strength), is considered the best, followed by filter coffee. In the morning people are not so keen on sweet cakes, but tend to eat croissants, preferably dry. Cakes are more for the afternoon, if at all. The highest praise for a cake is, 'very nice, not too sweet'.

Espresso coffee machines have become a status symbol. Most electrical shops carry models ranging from 200 to 1800 francs. You can usually hear the ones from the higher range from four streets away because they rev up and grind the beans so loudly. You can froth up the milk noisily with them too.

Chapter 11 Rules and social control

Ursula and her family moved into a townhouse complex with a small garden. They had their own driveway at the front leading to their garage, and she started hanging out her washing there, consisting mostly of diapers and baby clothes. She was surprised to get a letter from the management of the townhouse complex, saying it was not allowed to hang up washing outside. She was foreign and had no idea that this would be frowned upon. This story would be a good example of the stereotypical stories foreigners tell of strictly-regulated life in Switzerland, but Ursula is Swiss and the incident happened in Texas when she first moved there. It is not only in Switzerland that people are taken by surprise when they discover there are rules that make no sense to them. Whatever country you go and live in, you will find norms and expectations which are new to you. Ursula later learnt what was behind this concern about her washing, and she comments:

> I developed an understanding of the value system in that type of US middle class neighbourhood and realised that it was an expression of poverty to hang your washing up to dry at the front of the house. The dropping of standards could result in the dropping

of house prices. For the same reason house exteriors all looked smart at the front, although they might be falling to bits at the back.

An American family would have known that hanging up their washing at the front of that housing complex would make them look poor and lower the tone of the neighbourhood. The rule is explicit, but the reason for this rule is implicit knowledge which people who share the cultural norms think of as common sense. A further cultural issue may be the way rule infringement is dealt with. In Switzerland people believe it is better to be direct and tell people straight what they are doing wrong (although they do not always follow through on the ideal). This is dealt with in chapter 3.

Social control - for newcomers

'In Switzerland there seems to be a right time to be quiet or make a noise', a British mother commented to me, It took me a moment to realise she was talking about the rule that people should be quiet at lunch time. Switzerland doesn't come across as a typical siesta country, and it is hard to imagine the whole nation going to sleep in the middle of the day. However, there is usually a local by-law or house rule that you should not make a noise between 12 and 2 pm, (or after 10 pm, or on a Sunday), e.g. by cutting your grass, drilling holes or playing the piano. In English-speaking countries there is less of a clear break in the middle of the day.

It is not the case that everyone in Switzerland is just watching out for you to make a mistake. People who correct others are in the minority, but being corrected can be quite memorable to someone who is new in the country. Many Swiss people are surprised to hear that foreigners have been told off for disobeying rules. They don't notice the rules themselves because obeying them is second nature. Out of concern for the environment, they do not leave their car engine running while they run back into the house to get something. To avoid noise pollution, they do not mow their lawn after 7 pm on a Saturday evening, or at all on a Sunday. They do not let their toddlers run up and down on the tram (an unwritten rule). If you are foreign and have lived here for a long time, you will probably not be corrected very often for rule infringement either. It is typical of foreigners who have been here for years to believe Switzerland has changed a lot rather than themselves, because no one corrects them the way they used to. Graham Tritt, a New Zealander in Berne suggests you refresh your memory by sitting in your car and leaving the engine running and seeing how many people comment as they pass.

Air pollution is a cultural issue. In English-speaking countries people can get just as upset about smokers as Swiss people do about car exhaust fumes, and it is getting harder and harder to smoke in public places in some countries, even outdoors.

The challenge people face in moving to a new country is to familiarise themselves with the rules, written and unwritten, and develop an understanding of how these make sense in that culture. Ursula comments that in the USA there are more rules regarding safety compared to Switzerland, for example at a club pool or a production facility. These regulate details of behaviour which are left more to the individual in Switzerland.

In Switzerland many rules are related to space issues. People live very close together compared with other western countries and have to negotiate both the use of their space and noise levels. They are like other western countries in that they 'value their freedom', but with their limited space they put the emphasis on freedom from being disturbed by others, rather than the freedom to do as you please. Roger is Swiss and comments that in Switzerland people are very conscious of issues of space, and Swiss kids are brought up not to get into other people's space. (See also Chapter 24 on taking up space.)

A Swiss woman told me that when she came back to live with her parents in Switzerland after a year spent as an au pair in the USA, her mother complained that she was banging the garage door too loudly and that it would disturb the neighbours. She had obviously learned this habit in the USA, where houses are not built so close together. Noise is also an issue of shared space.

In Switzerland it is your duty not to disturb, just as in middle class areas of the USA it is your duty not to lower the prestige of the neighbourhood. Underlying this Swiss emphasis on duty is the concept of freedom, as expressed by Rousseau, a late 18th century Geneva-based philosopher. He was one of the original proponents of liberty, equality and brotherhood, but he advocated well-regulated freedom in the sense of one person's freedom ending where the next person's begins. This idea is alive and well today in Switzerland. (See also 'Etiquette as a duty' in the Appendix on politeness on page 226.)

Social control of children

Margaretha is Swiss, and has lived in both London and Glasgow. She believes that it is the task of the whole society, along with the parents, to help young people learn to become responsible adults:

> There is more explicit social control in Switzerland, which can be positive. People care and society has a duty to integrate the younger generation. People will admire babies, chat to children and also tell them off if necessary. My son Teddy annoyed a man by running back and forwards on a Swiss tram and so the man complained. I then noticed he wanted peace to talk on his mobile phone, and the Swiss part of me was tempted to say, 'You disturb people more with your mobile phone than my child does with his running!' However I have lived abroad a long time and have learned to restrain myself.

It is interesting that although Margaretha believes in the value of social control, if someone complains to her she still automatically felt like 'hitting back' by giving the man a piece of her mind. This is an instinctive reaction, and people's instinct to defend themselves in German-speaking Switzerland seems to be deeply ingrained.

I witnessed an old man complaining about a baby crying loudly on the bus in Basel, and the mother retorted in Swiss-German, 'There are institutions for old people like you who can't cope with the outside world'. In Switzerland the verbal 'hitting out' or 'hitting back' does not lead to violence, and instead often has the effect of putting grumblers in their place. (The same principle applies in some schools, where children are traditionally expected to hit back to get peace from the person hitting them). In Britain people are often afraid to speak out about other people's behaviour because it could escalate into a fist fight. They will mutter away to each other but not confront the people annoying them.

> In Britain, to avoid 'road rage' incidents escalating into physical fights, motorists are told not to look other drivers in the eye. In Switzerland road rage is almost unknown, and drivers are specifically advised to look other drivers in the eye to avoid accidents at crossroads, etc.

Although the man with the mobile phone just wanted peace to make a phone call, people also correct others because they genuinely care about how the young people of their society are turning out. They feel a sense of responsibility towards them, as Rudolf, a Swiss secondary school teacher in Canton St Gallen explains:

> It takes 'civil courage' to tell a young person to do something, for example to pick up their litter, because you are interfering with their freedom, but some of us feel we should intervene for society's sake. We have high environmental standards and we want to keep them.

His reference to civil courage comes from the German *Zivilcourage*, which, loosely translated, is a kind of citizen's courage, or the courage to stand up for your beliefs for the sake of the community.

Freshly baked parents

As Margaretha says, babies and small children get a lot of positive attention in Switzerland, with people admiring babies and chatting to children in public places. Children are excellent conversation starters for adults who feel they are otherwise not good at 'small talk'. I greatly appreciated people's kindness to my children, and have heard many other foreigners say the same. Some of the people who care about children will also be concerned that they are being treated well and brought up properly. Elderly people in particular may wish to assist in the education of inexperienced young parents (known in German as *frischgebacken*, or 'freshly baked'). Men out on their own with their babies are commonly accosted by old ladies because it is assumed that freshly-baked fathers are even more in need of assistance than freshly-baked mothers. Elderly ladies often expressed genuine concern to my husband that the baby would suffocate in the baby carrier he wore on his front. He just smiled benignly at them and let them peer in to see that her nose was free and she was still breathing. Other causes of concern are barefoot babies in summer, and babies with no hats or gloves on in winter (usually you have to explain patiently to the person concerned that they keep throwing them off).

Times are changing

Social control has its benefits, but those who care are increasingly a minority group. *Facts* magazine[25] reported that there were

40,000 video cameras installed in Switzerland, keeping an eye on people around the country, in particular in underpasses, underground car parks and at automatic teller machines outside banks (they didn't mention keeping an eye on barefoot babies in baby carriers). According to *Facts*, 'The authorities and companies install the optical spies where social control and trust in fellow-citizens have got lost'. The generation which is vigilant is getting older, and the country is changing.

On the tram again
Helen, a Scottish mother has also noticed that times are changing, and reports a journey on the tram with her eight-year-old daughter and two of her daughter's friends:
'They were sitting, laughing and giggling at the front of the tram, and an old man started complaining about them in Swiss German. We ignored him until, as we got off, he said in English, 'These are naughty children, not intelligent'. Then a Swiss lady, in her 40s, said in English, 'I apologise for him. He is very old. Do not worry about it.'

Swiss advertising

TV advertising can be a good guide to the values of a society, as was the case in the early 21st century with a new series of commercials on Swiss TV for Ricola herbal candy. The Swiss company Ricola, based in Laufen, Basel Land, ran an innovative series of commercials with story lines involving people from various countries who wanted to claim the glory for Ricola products.

"Who invented Ricola?" (Ricola TV commercial)

In the first advertisement, 'Finland', you see a group of Finnish men dressed in towels running around outside after their sauna. One of them boasts to his mates that he invented Ricola herbal sweets, and suddenly a very intense little Swiss man dressed in a suit appears and addresses him quite sharply, 'Who invented them?' 'The Swiss' the Finn admits. 'Who exactly?' the little man persists. 'Ricola!' the Finn replies (see photo above).

I asked Beat Kernen, the head of Communications at Ricola to explain the idea behind the controversial figure. He said the man was referred to within his communications department as a likeable '*Wadenbeisser*', literally a 'calf-biter', which in English could be called the 'ankle-nipper', as the equivalent of a harmless small dog which nips your ankles. They saw him as a likeable, gauche sort of guy, who wasn't out for anything for himself but only wanted the truth to be told about Ricola. He was not a policeman, which would mean a real authority figure, neither was he a concierge or caretaker, who has the rules and therefore power on his side. He came from the masses, was one of the people, and had no real power. He was courageous (civil courage again) because he stood up to male peer groups like the well-nourished Finns, and in later commercials, to cool Australian surfers and three mean-looking Mexicans.

Ricola's research on reactions to the commercial showed that the Germans liked the portrayal of the cute 'little brother'. Beat Kernen reported that it didn't mean much to the Americans, the Dutch understood it but didn't like it and the French were uncomfortable with the connotations of someone playing the policeman. It was then shown initially only in Germany and Switzerland. It increased Ricola sales significantly and polarised Swiss audiences as issues related to Switzerland's image tend to do.[26] The Ricola mailbag had never been so full. A certain number of comments were complaints about the commercial, saying it was small-minded, that they didn't like Swiss people being portrayed like the little man, or that it put Switzerland in a bad light. The majority who liked it generally thought he was very funny and some thought it was the best commercial they had ever seen.

The Swiss people I spoke to who liked it were usually fairly progressive and found the ankle-nipper in the commercial typical of a certain type of Swiss person they would not take too seriously in real life. Hans is Swiss and comments that people may also laugh to take the sting out of something that is potentially threatening, e.g. if being corrected makes them feel like a child again.

Negotiating real rules

Beat Kernen's comment on the ankle-nippers makes a useful distinction between whether people who correct you have any real authority behind them or whether they are doing it on the basis of what they think ought to be the rules. If they have a written rule to back them up, they have right on their side. However, even then it is sometimes possible to renegotiate the rules if you have a good reason. Check them out before you move in somewhere. If the rules say you cannot use the laundry room after 8 pm and you work till 7 pm, you could try asking for an exception to be made. It depends to a large extent on how assertive you are and who you are negotiating with.

If you have a young family who are used to a lot of space, you could try and find a house or apartment where there are also families around or at least where the neighbours lead busy lives and are not home all day. Visit the building at different times if you can, and note the noise levels. Try not to move in above retired people with time on their hands. I have heard countless stories of Swiss and foreign families in apartments having confrontations with stressed senior citizens who are home all day and disturbed by children skipping around in the apartment above them. If the house rules say you must be quiet between midday and 2 pm, they might expect you to keep to them.

Checking faults when you move in

When you move into a rented house or apartment you may be asked to make an inventory of defects. In an article on this subject for young people moving into their first apartment, *Brücken-bauer*, the Migros supermarket newspaper, recommends a bit of assertiveness when dealing with the landlord. 'Approach your landlord firmly but correctly (i.e. be well-mannered). Have no inhibitions about faulting anything. Otherwise you will have to pay for it when you move out. If the landlord does not want to make a list, make your own and send it immediately by registered post.'

Try to imagine you are getting the house ready for the Ideal Homes Exhibition, and then note everything that is not perfect, down to the bit of paint that has flaked off on the door frame.

Check things out with others

When you are familiarising yourself with the house rules and local community by-laws, be aware that you may not have to obey everything to the letter. How strictly rules are enforced depends on your neighbours (and whether there is a strict caretaker living in the house). Ursula suggests you check things out with a Swiss neighbour you get on well with. She lived in the USA for many years and believes there is no point in 'walking on eggs', not knowing what people might have problems with and guessing at what you might be able to get away with. She suggests:

It is best to talk to people in the same house to find out whether it would bother them if you played the piano between 12 and 2 because for some people it might not be a problem at all.

The problem for neighbours, especially older ones, may be your unpredictability as an exotic newcomer. Ursula suggests you reduce their uncertainty by giving them a chance to get to know you, chatting in the hallway, or over a cup of tea and most of them will be friendly in return. You can also reduce their uncertainty by telling them your plans. You may have read a rule telling you to be quiet after 10 pm, but it will probably still be okay to have a party in your apartment on a Saturday night. Some Swiss people let their neighbours know they are going to have a party that will go on late, and tell them when it will finish. Then if the neighbours are lying awake at midnight, at least they know it will be coming to an end at a specified time and do not have to fear it could go on all night.

Older people in particular worry about standards dropping and their living quality deteriorating, so showing you are aware of these issues will reassure them. This does not mean you have to do everything they want. You have rights too. If you think people are inventing new rules, you could say 'I missed that one' and ask them to show it to you in writing.

Dealing with 'ankle-nippers'

It helps if you can recognise whether people have real grounds for complaint, and if you cannot, do not take ankle-nippers seriously. School children learn to say 'Göschenen-Airolo' meaning 'in one ear and out the other' to reply to remarks made by others which are just not worth bothering about. (You enter the Gotthard tunnel in the village of Göschenen and come out the other side at Airolo).

Likewise it is good if you can just smile benignly at people who are nipping at your ankles.

It is interesting to hear Swiss people debate unwritten rules, e.g. whether there is a rule about how to pass others on the street. I was once corrected for walking on the left instead of the right of the pavement (sidewalk) and I discussed it with a group of postgraduate students. Some agreed with the supposed rule that you should keep to the right, while others said there is no rule. One man suggested you negotiate with each other where to walk by using eye contact, and a woman said that men walk straight down the middle of the pavement and women walk round them. It usually makes an interesting dinner party topic.

German reactions to rules

It is interesting for English-speaking foreigners to see how Germans deal with rules in Switzerland. Germans also come from a strongly rule-based society, but seem more likely than other foreigners[27] to question rules or recommendations by people in authority. Sally is British and describes an incident which illustrates different approaches of a British and a German mother to instructions from school:

At the beginning of the school year my daughter came home and told me she had to cover her maths books in red paper and her German books in blue paper. The colour coding was to help the children recognise and pack the correct books for homework at the end of the school day. We had no blue paper, and neither of the local supermarkets had any either, so in the end I had to buy a more expensive roll at the stationers. Then I ran into the German mother of a boy in my daughter's class, who told me she hadn't found blue paper in the supermarket so she just bought some striped paper with a bit of blue in it, and was sure that would be fine.

It comes more naturally to Germans than to Swiss to question 'authority' and judge for themselves whether a rule or stipulation makes sense. This may have its roots in early childhood. Ulrike Hoffmann-Richter, a German psychiatrist working in Switzerland, drew my attention to research conducted on the subject by Paul Parin, a Swiss-Yugoslav psychoanalyst. In 1976 Parin reported on a study comparing the way middle-class German and Swiss German mothers interact with their children.[28] If a child is making too much noise, the German mother will tell him to stop because she doesn't like it. The Swiss mother will tell the child it is not allowed, and refer to an outside authority which forbids it, such as the caretaker of the apartment block, the shopkeeper, etc. The German child can argue with the mother as the authority, but for the Swiss child it is not possible to argue with her about it because the mother is not the authority. She didn't make the rule.

Parin concluded that Germans learn much more to internalise their mother's expectations and norms and learn them for themselves, so that *they know by themselves what to do*. This gives them stiff internal standards but plenty of room for manoeuvre in the outside world.

> Parin also pointed out that when German parents get into arguments with their children about their instructions, they are also encouraging linguistic competence. This would mean that Germans learn early to develop a debating style. This is not generally the Swiss way (see chapter 17 on consensus).

It seems that many German Swiss still learn to refer primarily to an outside authority for guidance on how to behave throughout their lives. Some describe themselves as more 'adapted' (*angepasst*) than Germans because their environment exercises more authority over them. In comparison some Germans come across as extremely confident in Switzerland, or even a 'law unto themselves' because they are less influenced by others.

The Swiss tendency to let the environment exercise control over them can be hard for individualists to understand. It may be more easily understood by people from more collectivist, or group-oriented cultures, for example some in Asia. In collectivist societies, according to the psychologists Markus and Kitayama, mature adults are those who are able to think of their own personal needs as being secondary to the needs of the group. Giving in to another person's decision is not a passive or weak gesture, but is a sign of tolerance, self-control, flexibility and maturity.[29]

Historical reasons for social control

Where does this Swiss tradition of social control come from? Firstly, it is a very democratic way to behave. The rules belong to all the people, and it is the duty of all the people to see that they are kept. In Britain people have a bit of a 'them and us' mentality, linked with having a monarchy, an aristocracy and a class system, and do not feel so responsible for the common good. From a historical perspective there have been various influences in Switzerland which have long fostered a society with responsibility for the group in the hands of the people.

Religious perspective

According to the Swiss scholar Albert Debrunner, the view that rules should be enforced by the people has its roots in the Calvinist tradition. The Protestant reformer Calvin was an important historical influence in the 1540s, turning Geneva into a 'Protestant Rome'. As the ultimate teacher of duties he laid down strict laws of conduct, (e.g. only two meals a day, meat twice a week, evening curfews, etc.) and had people checked on by the elders in their homes as to whether they were obeying. Zurich was also strictly Protestant under Zwingli, e.g. people couldn't leave the city on a Sunday. Zwingliism and Calvinism were both characterised by communitarianism, in which it is not the priest who decides, but the whole group.

Calvinist countries

Other Calvinist countries, like Scotland and the Netherlands also used to exercise more social control. The well-known nursery rhyme 'Wee Willie Winkie' makes reference to the evening curfew in Glasgow: 'Are all the children in their beds? It's past eight o'clock'.

In Holland nowadays people still leave the curtains open in their living rooms, so that everyone can see what they are doing. Many Dutch people refer to this as a custom which originated in the days of control by the church elders, who wanted to see what people were doing in their homes.

Rights and responsibilities

The reason that rules have continued to be so important in Switzerland is that when the new Swiss federal state was formed in 1848, the cantons of Zurich and Geneva were economically dominant and the liberal federal state took over a lot of their Protestant standards. So rules with a religious basis became rules for general conduct all over the country. This makes for a well-regulated society with social and political control mechanisms in the hands of the people. Everyone understands their rights and responsibilities, and citizenship includes taking them seriously. The voting system reinforces this. The local communities, rather than the cantonal government or central government make the decisions on many issues. People are used to feeling responsible for all aspects of community life.

Section three: Children and culture

Chapter 12   Fostering self-reliance

When my daughter started Swiss playgroup at the age of three, I attended my first Swiss parents' evening. I was surprised when the leader said one of their aims was to help children to learn to play alone, as modern children were not so good at this as they should be. This was my introduction to Swiss pedagogical principles. I had realised that Swiss mothers who still washed their windows weekly would have less time to play with their toddlers or organise activities such as finger-painting for early learning. However I hadn't realised until then that the professionals would recommend leaving children to play alone.

This chapter takes a look at differences in beliefs about good parenting with regard to play. Different attitudes can be found between parents and professionals within German-speaking Switzerland. Birgit is Scandinavian and describes an incident when she was in Bern, visiting her Swiss brother-in-law Daniel, his Swiss wife Ruth, who is a kindergarten teacher, and their two-year-old daughter Julia.

Julia was building a house, and when the bricks all toppled down, her dad made a move to go and help her. Ruth said, 'No, leave her!' and he went and sat down again. I was quite startled. Ruth is a kindergarten teacher and believes you should let the child do this sort of thing alone, as a learning experience. I am a primary school teacher, but I would also have helped Julia. That's my instinct.

Swiss child-development professionals believe parents should not interfere in their children's play, although, as can be seen from Daniel's reaction, Swiss parents do not necessarily hold these beliefs to the same degree.

Professor Remo Largo is a leading German Swiss paediatrician and an authority on child development. In his book *Kinderjahre,*[30] he writes that parents should let their children learn for themselves, giving an example of 18-month-old Karl, who tries to build a tower with different sized plastic beakers. After many failed attempts, Karl discovers you have to stack them in order of size, and finally gets it right. Through this experience of finding the solution to the problem on his own, Karl discovers he is capable of solving problems, and gains confidence in his ability to master difficult situations in the future too.

Largo emphasises that it is not what the child learns but how it learns that is important. The developmental issue is: 'Can the child develop learning and problem-solving strategies?' He sees parental involvement in play as interference. If parents interfere, they are teaching the child, 'We always know better than you. Ask us if you need help'. If he does ask for help, they should try and do as little as necessary, to help him to continue independently (the German word *selbständig* can be translated more accurately as 'self-reliantly').

> A question of semantics
> Where English speakers say 'intervention' or 'involvement', Swiss Germans often use the word 'interference'. It can be interference in play, or when children are fighting, as is shown later in the chapter. This can also be an issue in the international workplace if the Anglo American boss's involvement is experienced as interference by the Swiss employee (see chapter 26.)

In contrast to the hands-off approach expected of Swiss parents, for many middle-class English-speaking parents, usually mothers, child-rearing is a much more demanding task and they might feel guilty if they don't have time to play with their children. This is a particular pressure if they have left their roots and have no extended family in the same region or country providing practical and moral support. A mother may then be her child's sole daytime companion and if she believes the English-language childcare books, it is important that she takes an active part in her child's development. For example, in a British practical guide for parents, Shakuntala Devi[31] recommends to parents to be a partner in play:

> Be a partner: As a parent you have the maturity and insight to know what your child will benefit from, and you want your child to have the best. By perceiving her individual needs, interests and abilities, you can introduce variety.
> Research conducted on the parent-child playing relationship has come up with some interesting findings . . . children who play

regularly with their parents are more likely to achieve the highest
level of creativity as adults.

Karl's tower and the world of work

From Largo's point of view, the main gain for Karl in building
his tower is that he develops confidence in his problem solving
ability. However I can't help noticing that with his efforts made
on his own, he has also gained a thorough knowledge of the exact
process required to achieve the goal. It could be that if an adult
helped Karl, he would achieve the goal of producing a beaker
tower, but still wouldn't know the steps, (or procedures) required
to achieve it the next time. This rings bells for me with regard to
problems business clients have described in international project
work. In working towards a goal, a recurring problem is that German-speaking Swiss and Germans want to have procedures defined clearly, while for Anglo-Americans it doesn't matter so
much how you get there, as long as you get there (see Jeannette's
story in chapter 26). Clearly-defined concepts and procedures to
be followed are not so important.

Young children fighting

The issue of self-reliance also arises in connection with the degree to which adults should intervene in children's fights. Jeanne
Darling, Director of Tiny Tots Day Care Centre in Basel, describes
a difference she notices there between the Swiss staff and herself:

I've had discussions with Swiss day-care staff who say 3-year-
old kids will work out their quarrels on their own. Take for example a tussle over a truck. If Simon has a truck, and I see Mark grab-

bing it from him, I will stop Mark and say, 'you need to ask Simon for the truck. You don't just grab it', and then I say to Simon, 'if you don't like his taking it, you need to say no'. I'm intervening. The Swiss level of intervention is at the point of injury, whereas mine is at the point where Simon backs down, because he needs to learn to defend himself. I believe Mark needs to learn not to bully his way through. There are better means to get what one wants.

In Switzerland there is a more hands-off mentality when children interact than in many English-speaking societies. Swiss children are allowed to play more independently at a younger age without adults watching closely what they are doing. Cathy, a Swiss American based in Geneva, commented that in the playground near her home she was the only mother who was constantly chasing after her toddler, telling him not to hit other kids. The other mothers sat and chatted to each other and did not enter into their children's play, or get involved if they hit each other, unless things got nasty. In Switzerland children are supposed to deal with minor skirmishes among their peers by themselves and can hit back in self-defence if someone hits them (although Esther Kubli, a Swiss primary school teacher, suggests that the child being hit should first try firmly telling the other child to stop).

Hitting back is a problem for children (including Swiss children) who have been educated in English-speaking countries with a policy of zero-tolerance of violence. Their parents and teachers there have taught them not to hit back but rather to first ignore children harassing them, and if it continues, to report it to a teacher. One English mother commented, 'Kids have to learn to be tough in Switzerland'.

Toughening up my children was not on my list of priorities as a mother, but because my children went to Swiss playgroups, they learned to stand up for themselves without me really noticing. When my daughter was two years old, she went to a Swiss playgroup where Irene, the leader, told the ten children a story while they jumped on an old mattress. I asked Irene once how my daughter was getting on and Irene replied that she was doing fine and was well able to assert herself among the kids.

I remembered this incident down the years because I was surprised that assertiveness was considered a developmental issue worthy of mention for a two-year-old. When I was writing this book, I wondered how exactly she had been asserting herself and phoned Irene. She explained that the children had queued for their turn jumping on the mattress, and if someone pushed in front of my daughter, she would push back to defend her place in the queue. If other children got too close jumping, my daughter would also push them away.

Creating conflicts
Switzerland is by no means extreme in its hands-off child-rearing style. There was an interesting study of three to five-year-olds in a Japanese (Buddhist) pre-school[32] in which the teacher did not get involved in conflicts at all. It was explained that as the term progressed, the teachers even removed some of the toys to create conflicts so that the children had to learn to share!

Chapter 13   Self reliance and school

Ursula and Walter are Swiss, but spent nine years in the USA, where their children first attended school. When they returned to Switzerland the children went into first and second grade of Swiss school. Ursula was struck by how German Swiss school children were raised to be responsible for themselves much earlier than in the USA:

> In Switzerland what they have to do for homework isn't always written down, so the parents can't check if what the child is reporting at home is correct. It's something between the children and the teacher. They have to know what homework to do, do it on their own and bring it to school on time.
>
> Children walk to school on their own. They are not driven there. They have to be responsible in traffic really early. This was a real change for our children when they got here. It took them a while to learn it.

Ursula's examples are fairly typical of German Swiss schools, but because schools and individual teachers are all so different, there are some variations too. Some teachers may ask the children to make a note of the homework exercise, and a few may suggest to parents how they can do extra maths work with their children.

Few teachers expect parents to have any responsibility for the homework. One teacher commented that mistakes in the homework gave her valuable feedback as to whether the children understood what they had been learning in class. This was helpful to me to understand *why* I should not correct my daughter's homework.

Teachers usually recommended that children walk to school alone, or with their friends. It is an opportunity to be responsible for themselves in the outside world without adult supervision. Parents practise walking the route with them and a policeman gives them training in crossing the road at kindergarten and school. German Swiss parents express little fear of children having problems with traffic or crime. In the French and Italian-speaking parts of the country there seems to be more of a desire to protect children, and a few Swiss parents I spoke to there made references to the potential dangers of crimes against children.

Every year when school starts, there are many posters in the German-speaking part of the country warning drivers to watch out for the children who are walking to school or kindergarten alone for the first time (see illustration). The slogan used in 2001, *Gäll, du bassisch uff mi uff* can be roughly translated 'You'll watch out for me,

won't you', or perhaps 'You'll look after me, won't you?'[33] The implications seem to be that parents are not only giving up the child to school but to society (in the form of drivers) to take care of, and in this poster the child is displaying an attitude of trust.

A citizen of the big wide world

> 'Are you ready to symbolically authorise your children to go to school, that is, to leave the family home and in a sense go out into the big wide world? If you can't answer 'yes' to this question, ask yourself why it is so difficult for you.'[34]

This was a question asked on the Etat de Genève (State of Geneva) website for families on the subject of children starting school. In German the word *Ablösung* (separation or detachment) is commonly used by teachers and parents to refer to the separation which should take place at this time. German Swiss also talk about starting kindergarten or school in terms of 'giving away' the child and, as in the website, they refer to the children 'going out' into the world. This does not seem to be expressed in such a clear cut way in English. English speakers tend to believe the biggest milestone in separating and detaching from their child should be when their child becomes a grown up and is ready to leave home. *Swiss News* magazine[35] quotes Laurie Hubermann, an American who finds it surprising that Swiss university students still sleep in their childhood beds all through their studies:

> The US college experience provides an excellent transition between childhood and adulthood. If you go to university and live

at home, you have trouble making a move toward adulthood, because you are stuck in the context of your childhood. It's not good for a 24- or 25- year old to still be at home.

Dan Daniels is a professor of biomedical engineering from the USA who now works in Switzerland as a consultant. He comments from his experience as a US student, parent and professor:

Most students in the US start college at about 18, and more live at home during their first few college years than the opposite. However, many US parents believe their children will benefit from going away to college at this age, if the resources are available for them to do so. Also, those who stay at home for a first college degree leave home (and often also their home city) at about age 22 or so, if they decide to embark on post-graduate or professional studies.

Swiss parents are less likely to see benefits to leaving home as early as 18. However, if their children are still living at home after the age of 25, Swiss parents may start to be concerned. Many people think that it is then time for children to leave 'Hotel Mama' and start looking after themselves.

Home from home

School is a 'home from home' to a greater extent in German-speaking Switzerland than in English-speaking cultures. Yannis, a German Swiss six-year-old boy drew a picture of his new school for a newspaper article on starting school[36] (see illustration on the following page). There is smoke coming out the chimney and it is in effect a picture of a house. The word *Schulhaus* is used in German (as he wrote on the roof). In English the schoolhouse is where the teacher lives, and the building where classes are held is just called the 'school'.

School by Yannis

At both Swiss kindergarten and the first few years of school, when children sit on benches in a circle to talk or eat or sing together, it is called the *Stübli* (little living room). Children have the same class teacher for at least two years, and often four years. It is a more long-term relationship than in countries in which children have the same teacher for one year only. The teacher becomes very important in children's lives, and gets to know them very well in the years they are together.

Parents usually visit the school for parents' evenings and occasionally sit in on class, but it is unusual for the parents to stay and help the teacher, e.g. with reading practice or handicrafts, as is often done in English-speaking cultures. A Swiss mother would no more think of helping out at school than she would offer to help the doctor give children their vaccinations at the local surgery.

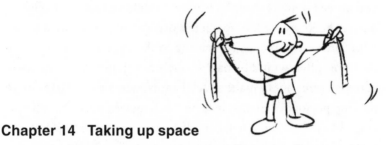

Chapter 14   Taking up space

How much physical and psychological space should you give your children? All around the western world children are more the focus of attention than their parents and grandparents were, but if you compare different cultures, there are still marked differences. This subject was brought up in an interview with Ursula, a Swiss mother who lived in the USA for nine years:

> Kids have different standing in Swiss society compared to the USA. There, a child is elevated to a special status, and is taken very seriously. In Switzerland a child is raised to become a part of society but is not the most important part. Adults, especially working adults, are more important. You honour older people. Kids are expected to fit in and are not given extra privileges. For a long time in restaurants, nothing was available to entertain or accommodate kids, no playgrounds or high chairs. It is only recently that trains and restaurants have started to do this.

As well as provisions for children in public places, Ursula's comments are also relevant to the degree to which Swiss parents 'childproof' their homes to make them child-centred. I followed the instructions of the British baby books and parents' magazines and moved objects like plants out of reach, so that we would not have to keep saying 'no' to our children when they wanted to play with forbidden objects. According to the experts, saying 'no' to them too often would be bad for their development. Some Swiss parents prefer not to make special adjustments and apart from removing poisonous plants, instead teach their babies or toddlers to keep away from the plants, and have respect for the glass coffee table. (They then take their children out to the park to run around and let off steam). It seemed that both ways are teaching the child something about the world, either preparing them to expect a world with a minimum of restrictions or else a world in which restrictions exist and are to be managed. I believe both ways are valid steps towards socialisation, according to the culture the child is integrating into.

Seating arrangements

Early experiences out and about in the world can also give a child (and its parents) messages about its place in society. Even seating arrangements can convey a message. At an English-language mother and toddler's group I attended, the mothers sat on armchairs lining the walls, and the main area in the middle was designated for the children, to give them maximum playing space. It was soon a blanket of toys. The mothers were constantly watching their children, and some of their conversations centred around the way they were playing. As well as getting to know each other, the mothers tended to take an interest in the behaviour and temperaments of each other's children. In contrast, in a Swiss mother and toddler's group I attended, the mothers sat in the middle of the room round a table, and the children played on a cloth on the floor with toys on it at the side of the table. Many of the mothers did not watch their children unless they attracted their attention in some way, and then they turned round from the table to see what they were doing. They chatted about their own children, but did not observe or discuss the way they were playing at that moment. If a child wanted her mother, she went and sat on her lap, away from the other children and the toys.

Both groups could be roughly defined as middle-class. At the Swiss group, the children had to choose between their mothers and the other children with the toys. The English-speaking children could have the attention of their mothers, play with each other and the toys, and perhaps also involve their mothers in playing too. The English-speaking group clearly had more 'child-centred' seating arrangements, giving the children both more space and more attention than at the Swiss group. However, superficial aspects like seating arrangements alone do not dictate how people are meant to interact with each other. Helen is Scottish and describes what happened at a mother and toddlers' group in England where mothers sat around a table, Swiss-style, drinking their coffee:

> Sitting at the table was OK for mums sitting at the end nearest to their child but those at the other end couldn't easily see what their children were doing and very soon migrated down to the floor beside them (leaving their coffee behind). If you were a mum still left at the table, you could easily feel you were neglecting your child.

Parenting in a context

Parents bring up their children in a context, not a vacuum. In any culture there are expectations of what good parenting is, (and what is bad and neglectful) and parents, especially mothers, are influenced by their environment. In Helen's example the seating arrangements were not child-centred enough for that group of mothers and so most of them ended up on the floor beside their children.

I experienced the importance of children joining adults at the table in Switzerland one summer when our older daughter was two. We were visiting relatives, and our daughter had been given a lot of crisps (potato chips) by friendly uncles when we arrived, and so we knew she wouldn't be hungry for dinner. We figured she would be difficult to entertain at the table, which was in the garden, and decided to take turns accompanying her on her explorations of the garden (the child-centred approach). My husband wandered off with her, but then had to return quite fast because the group refused to start dinner without them. We tried to explain that she was not hungry and would be happier ambling around the garden. We said that we would both in turn be able to eat in peace without her, but they just could not comprehend why anyone, regardless of age, would not be joining them at the table when it was time to eat. So she sat at the table, and as far as I remember, she made quite a mess playing with her food, but was entertained by all the people talking to her.

In Switzerland the whole family eating together at the same time (at a table) is more important than in many English-speaking cultures. Swiss children seem to be better able to sit longer at the table, probably because it is 'just expected' and they sense this. Now that I have observed this for so many years, perhaps I would 'just expect it' of my grandchildren too.

Space issues in kindergarten

A child's understanding of its place in society is also an aspect of social competence, which is emphasised in Swiss kindergarten and school. Every child should have a sense of belonging, and of his or her place. This may involve not taking up too much space. Lila Buchs, a Basel-based teacher trainer and coach for educators and parents, explains that social competence is developed at kindergarten as children learn to have rapport with others, and listen to each other without interrupting:

> Socialisation involves, among other things, not letting children take up too much space. Learning to restrain yourself is important because your freedom stops where the freedom of the other starts. A kindergarten teacher who is handing something out will often not give first to the 'gimme' ('give me') person, but to the quiet child who is standing back, behaving well. Children learn to be modest and show consideration. They learn that the interests of the other are as important as their own, although different teachers stress this to a different degree. The Anglo-Saxon way is to stand up in front of a group. We Swiss are more likely to feel we have to explain why we are standing out like that and excuse ourselves by saying, 'I'm here because I have been asked to say something' to show that we wouldn't do it of our own accord.

Presentation training in kindergarten

Swiss business people often comment with envy on the ability of English speakers to stand in front of a group and make presentations with great ease. Paul, an Englishman who had worked in Canada, commented in one of my courses that Canadian children get early training with the custom of 'show and tell', in which they bring some kind of object to pre-school and stand in front of the others and talk about it. They are encouraged to take their turn at standing out.

When a child has been used to a very child-centred approach, and has not attended a Swiss group before, it is not only the language which has to be learned. Depending on the child's personality, the teacher may report that he wants too large a 'share of the pie', or too much of her attention, and is not willing to 'stand back'. This can sound alarming, so it may be helpful to ask the teacher for specifics: what exactly is your child doing, and what exactly would she like him to be doing? Ask permission to sit in on the group time and ask her to interpret your child's behaviour afterwards. Then tell her how it looks to you. Over the two years or so, he is likely to adjust to the behaviour of the other kindergarten children and take up less space. The Swiss children are learning it too, but probably already have the internal cultural programming to grasp more quickly what is wanted. Ask for your child to be given more time to adjust.

There are pros and cons to all kinds of cultural skills. If your child likes talking a lot, and taking centre stage, she will probably be great at speaking to a group one day, which is not an easy skill for many Swiss people. At the same time, it is useful for a child growing up in Switzerland to learn the local values in order to be comfortable in the culture. Children who know how to find their place in the group are children who feel they belong.

Section four: The world of work

Chapter 15   English in international companies

What percentage of Swiss staff sometimes speak English at work? 20%? 40%? Or even 80%? If you work in a very international environment, and you can only speak English, you might get the impression that most people are speaking English every day, because the people you meet are speaking it to you. In fact every fifth employee speaks English at work[37] in Switzerland. It is quite an achievement that they can. As mentioned in chapter 6, most people learn English as a third or even fourth language in Swiss schools, and many have to attend evening classes to bring their English up to a standard they can use in their daily work.

How many people speak French at work in London or New York? 1%? 2%? 5%? It's probably not many. Try to imagine a situation where, due to shifts in the world economy, the working language in UK and US companies changes to French over a period of years. English-speaking staff have to dust off their school French and attend language classes to learn basic grammar and vocabulary. At management level they go to Paris for exclusive training courses in making presentations, writing e-mails, using the phone, leading a meeting, performing well in French at interviews, and possibly negotiating in French too. If they are writing to English-speaking co-workers and sending a copy to the French boss, the mail has to be written in French because she can't speak English.

Once they have all invested hundreds of hours and thousands of pounds or dollars in their language training, they are back in their home country, faced with Parisians, Canadians, Belgians and colleagues from the south of France all in the same meeting, speaking very quickly with different accents, using colloquialisms and slang words. Some seem to be swallowing the ends of their words so that they are incomprehensible even to advanced learners.

This shift of language is basically what happened in various companies in Switzerland in the 80s and 90s with regard to English. Swiss company language policy is very accommodating to highly qualified foreigners compared to many cultures, and perhaps their international business success can be partly attributed to this. Switzerland is often competing with the USA to attract the best scientists, marketing specialists, and IT staff from around the world. The international companies know that they could not attract these high flyers to Switzerland if learning to work in German or French was part of the deal. The USA would then be much more attractive. Instead, many Swiss companies have made English their official language. Expatriate staff who do not speak the local language may be offered free language classes, but are only expected to learn the language for an hour or two a week. It is up to the local Swiss staff to be able to speak English.

Some Swiss staff are happy to have the challenge of working in a foreign language in their home country, but the fact that they do so should not be taken for granted. The contrast becomes obvious if an employee joins a Japanese company and works in Tokyo. He could easily be required to spend his first two months in a full-time day and night immersion language programme, and the same could apply in France, Italy or Spain, as Swiss managers sometimes report.

> Comparisons with Italy and Japan
> Armin, a German scientific manager told me that he went from Swiss headquarters to give training to staff in the Italian affiliate. They listened to his input in English, but then discussed the new information in Italian, so that Armin had no idea what they were saying. When he gave training in Japan he knew most of the staff couldn't speak English, so at my suggestion, he set up little groups for discussion in Japanese, each with a spokesperson who would translate the feedback back to him in English. Neither of these scenarios would happen in Switzerland. If staff joined a team where training was going to be given in English, they would all either already speak it (as a prerequisite to joining the team), or head off to enrol for intensive language classes to learn it fast.

Because everyone in international teams in Swiss companies seems to speak good English, it should be possible to work effectively in English alone. In practice it is not quite so easy, although Swiss staff may not admit it openly. The situation with in-company English in Switzerland is similar to the imaginary example with different varieties of French. Even for a fluent non-native speaker, it is not easy to understand the different accents of English from all over the world. Meetings are not as effective as they should be because people do not want to keep repeating that they don't understand. It can be assumed that this is a great cause of inefficiency in certain pockets of many companies. Many people attend English classes in the hope of improving their listening skills. This can take a long time because of all the different accents of English which have to be understood. It is much easier for non-native speakers if native speakers practise speaking a simplified version of their own language.

Keep it simple
I heard a BBC TV newsreader ask a non-native speaker studio guest, 'Did you manage to form an independent opinion as to how many people have died?' The guest hesitated, as he tried to work out what the question meant. That wasted quite a bit of time on air. An easier way would have been to make two questions: 'What do you think? How many people have died?'

It takes a bit of skill and practice to simplify your English, but it should still be less demanding than the few hundred hours needed to learn English as a foreign language. Will it help if you slow down, pronounce all the words very clearly, or simplify your sentences? Not being able to use your language the way you do with 'the folks back home' can be accompanied by a sense of loss that you cannot be as eloquent as you like, or use your favourite colloquialisms or subtle humour. This is the case for non-native speakers to a greater degree, as they cannot even speak simply (or use subtle humour) in their mother tongue at all when speaking to you.

In a report on a Swiss bank which branched out into investment banking, and had many new English speaking employees as a result, a German Swiss employee is quoted as saying:

> We can all speak good English, but we can never speak as spontaneously, humorously, with originality and as convincingly as most of us can in German.

He went on to say that it was a disadvantage for Swiss staff that they did not usually manage to reply within the 'required tenth of a second'.[38] This raises the question of 'interrupting'. Probably the English speakers were much more willing to interrupt each other than the Swiss, who felt that if they didn't speak in the crucial tenth of a second, they had lost their chance until the next break in the conversation, if it ever came. These communicative issues are often taboo topics, but it may be worthwhile for team leaders to put them on the agenda for discussion in order to increase the efficiency of international meetings and team work.

Chapter 16 Plain speaking as an ideal

Christoph is Swiss and joined the English company Zeneca just before they merged with the Swedish company Astra. After the merger, he noticed certain differences in communication styles, as the following example shows:

If the Swedes came up with an idea in a project team meeting, the English might say, 'Mm, interesting.' The Swedes took this literally at first, and thought their proposal had been received positively. In fact for the English, 'interesting' meant the suggestion was a bit strange and this was a polite way of expressing it.

Mary is from the USA and says she was taught to say 'interesting' when she had nothing else (meaning, nothing positive) to say. Larry, who is also from the USA, comments that it also gives people time to think about a reply. It is a non-committal response. Like the Swedes, German Swiss are unlikely to make a comment like 'Interesting . . .' if they don't agree with an idea. They would either say nothing (see below) or say they disagree.

Silence is golden

In an in-company intercultural training course I asked the participants to divide into groups according to nationality to discuss the meaning of silence. The Japanese group reported back that they would be silent in a meeting as a sign of respect for what someone had just said, or if they didn't agree.

The British/South African group said silence suggested that they had nothing to say, i.e. no ideas, and the Swiss group said it would probably mean they didn't agree.

German Swiss often use silence to avoid conflict with others, rather than express disagreement in a roundabout way.

Different ideals

What do you say when your colleagues invite you to go for a drink after work, and you don't want to go? Some German Swiss report that they might say they 'can't come' but feel it is cowardly behaviour, and that ideally they *should* say they 'don't want to come', for the sake of honesty and clarity. They have a conflict between the ideal of 'telling the truth' and the practicalities of 'avoiding conflict with colleagues' (and silence doesn't work here because an answer is required).

> Honesty as a cause of tension
> The different approaches to honesty can cause tension in intercultural relationships. Heidi said her honesty in a relationship was causing conflict with her English friend who was hurt by it, and she would have to consider whether it was worth preserving the relationship if she could not be her true self.

In Anglo-American cultures people say they 'can't come', if they don't want to come, in order not to hurt others' feelings.

Making a polite excuse (which may not be quite true) is considered socially acceptable behaviour in most English speaking cultures, and is a necessity in some Asian cultures if you want a relationship to continue.

Armchair idealism and container pragmatism

German Swiss have particular expressions to refer to straight talking, often connected with the German language. Taking *'Klartext'* ('clear text') and *'Deutsch und deutlich'* ('German and clearly') as well as *'auf Deutsch gesagt'* ('said in German') are all used in the way in English we refer to 'calling a spade a spade', and not 'beating about the bush'.

Young people seem to be quite fond of plain speaking. Perhaps it is the idealism of youth. This came to light in the first Swiss Big Brother programme on Swiss TV3 in the autumn of 2000 which featured twelve German Swiss under the age of 35 living in a container together. One of the twelve contestants, Conny, was very outspoken and regularly gave the others a piece of her mind. She was unpopular with her co-habitants because of it, but the mostly young viewers appreciated her directness and finally voted that she should leave the container only on the last night. Remo, another contestant, was unpopular with the viewers because he was always talking about the others behind their backs in the garden. However, he was popular with his co-habitants because they didn't experience his criticism directly and found him easy to live with.

There was disparity between the 'armchair idealism' of the viewers, who prioritised honesty, open conflicts and clarity (embodied in Conny) and the 'container pragmatism' of the inhabitants, most of whom prioritised a peaceful life and avoiding direct confrontation (an approach embodied in Remo). Both of these types of communication can be experienced in Switzerland, as this and the following chapter show.

Ariane reports: In the business world in the French part of Switzerland, the more the discussions are related to internal politics, the less direct the communication will be. You can be outspoken when dealing with minor subjects, but will have to apply a more circular diplomacy, not to say a *langue de bois* ('language of the wooden tongue', i.e. talking in a rigid way, without really saying anything), when dealing with sensitive issues, as this example demonstrates:

Didier had just taken up a six-month ad-interim job as head of department during the sabbatical leave of his boss. This department was the product of a recent merger, and things were not yet operating as people expected. Four weeks into his mandate, he was invited by the management of operations to take part in a meeting to explain the nature and cause of the prevailing problems. He was encouraged by his superior to be as honest as possible. The participants seemed to be pleased with his sincere presentation, and many thanked him in private for his frankness. But two weeks later, he could feel that management was hesitating to take the actions he had proposed and they had seemed to support. When he enquired, a member of management told him in confidence: 'Never be honest, direct and sincere - even if you're asked for it'.

Giving instructions

How directly do staff go about telling each other what to do in Switzerland? Imagine you are a publications manager and have to get your company in-house magazine ready to send to the printer's on Friday. Some colleagues still haven't sent you their articles. You are now sending an e-mail to remind them and have various choices as to how to go about it.

1. You could be very direct and to the point and say: 'The magazine is going to the printer's on Friday. Please send your article immediately!' This is clear and to the point, and preferred by some German Swiss.

2. A second option might be to introduce an element of respectful politeness, and say 'I would appreciate it if you could send your article by Friday as a matter of urgency'. Some German Swiss may use this one, but others would be concerned that it is not clear whether this is a request or an order. Saying 'I would appreciate it if . . .' is introducing a personal element, which is a less efficient way to communicate. It is not clear that the reader has to send the article.

3. Thirdly, you could go for the personal touch, (using politeness strategies of involvement - see chapter 2), as was reported to me by Roger, an American publications manager: 'I'm going to be in trouble if I don't get the

magazine off to the printer's by Friday. Could you please send me your contribution immediately'. Another variation would be to refer to the person's situation: I know you must be really stressed just now, but could you please... These would both be a bit too personal for most German Swiss.

4. Lastly, you could be really indirect, as was reported by an English woman who worked for a publishing house in London. Her boss would just say, 'The magazine is going to the printer's on Friday'.

It would be considered an order if the boss merely sent out this kind of message. Everyone would then rush to get their articles ready for publishing. They knew the boss, and the situation, and therefore knew to interpret the message as an order. A new staff member might make the mistake of saying 'so what?' Indirect messages can be seen as inefficient in Swiss business, and unnecessary if the matter being discussed is not meant to be 'personal'. (See also chapter 3, 'It's not personal'.)

Clarifying authority

In a study of internal e-mail in Swiss banks, Ulla Kleinberger Günther[39] noted that in intranet communication within a large company, it is not always clear who is authorised to give instructions, and who has to carry them out. She explains direct instructions as a strategy used to increase clarity:

Directives which are formulated in a 'direct and dry' manner seem to be successful and cause the least misunderstandings.

In the specific constellation of the internet in daily business, 'politeness' is relegated by 'clarity' to a secondary role in the interest of the recipient knowing precisely what she has to do.

She gives an example in German *Ich erwarte noch die Folien von dir*, which is a very difficult expression to translate accurately. The words literally mean: 'I still expect the transparencies from you', but they also carry the connotations of, 'You were supposed to have sent them'. In industry I have often seen people write what may be a looser translation: 'I'm still waiting for the transparencies'. This may come across as a bit impatient in English. Keep in mind that if you receive a mail like this from a German speaker, it could just be an unfortunate translation of a standard phrase in German. There may also be an issue of authority which needs to be clarified. They may think if they risk asking you to do something, with a 'Could you please…', that you will treat it as a real question and say no.

In the English affiliate of a Swiss company, people told me they were upset about the direct messages they sometimes received from their Swiss headquarters. They called these stroppograms, from the English word stroppy meaning angry (*hässig* in Swiss German). It was probably due to an under-use of polite expressions, like 'Could you..' expected by the English.

Trusting words

One advantage of the Swiss ideal of telling the truth is that people's words can be trusted, and do not need to be interpreted. This can be of great value in communication. Many English-speaking foreigners living in Switzerland get used to this way of communicating too, and expect others to 'trust their words'. Sandy is South African and has lived for many years in Switzerland. She reports that her brother-in-law, Tom, in South Africa wanted to sell a piece of land, and so she told him on the phone that she definitely wanted to buy it. She was just getting ready to send the money, when, to her surprise, she heard from a brother that he had sold it to someone else. Tom had not been sure she would really buy it. Her words had not been enough.

Chapter 17   Consensus and internal politics

German and Swiss contrasts

Sabine is a psychologist who grew up bilingual in Germany, speaking High German with her German father and a Swiss German rural dialect with her Swiss mother. She now lives in Switzerland and feels the difference within herself when she is speaking one of the two languages:

> When I am speaking German I am less friendly, and more direct. When I am speaking Swiss German I am more friendly and less direct. Germans tend to be confrontational and Swiss avoid confrontation. The Swiss are more adaptable, compromise- and consensus-oriented.

It has been mentioned in previous chapters that German Swiss can criticise, give instructions or correct people very directly, when they see something as a technical issue rather than a personal matter. However, when they are asking for something, and the issue has 'political' implications (in the sense of power politics), they tend to be more cautious as to how they approach it. Sabine thinks her Swiss partner, a manager in a young Swiss company, has a typical Swiss approach:

> The Swiss act more slowly, while the Germans are three times faster. If a German wants financing for a project he will get on the phone and say, 'I want this, this and this'. The Swiss says a few nice things first. My Swiss partner is a prototype: I listen to him on the phone and wonder, 'When is he going to get to the point?' But this caution works better in Switzerland. He is checking things out, keeping in mind what the other person may want, what the possibilities are. In the end he says, 'Could you perhaps...?' It is less definite than in German. A solution is then negotiated.

The Swiss preference for consensus is central to their approach to decision-making. It is best known from the realm of politics. Ulrich Rubli, an employee of a Swiss pharmaceutical company, describes it as follows:

> The Swiss political system was created by the people and represents their way of thinking. Our consensus is based on compromises, which is vital to our survival as a country, otherwise we cannot co-exist as three or four different cultures. We need a common platform, and we are open to the idea that every opinion may have something right about it. We hesitate to say someone else is absolutely wrong and do not want to just defend our own point, ignoring the other perspective. In our political system we do not have 'the government versus the opposition'. The country is governed by 'concordance' or the agreement of seven representatives of all the main political parties. If a party takes a totally controversial stance, it will make it difficult to maintain the common platform long-term.

Steve Pawlett is Canadian and runs 'be', a business English training company. He comments:
One of the things I like about Swiss people is their fantastic and infuriating ability to compromise. Never have I looked at so many sides of an issue while discussing things.

Not a debating culture

Taking a controversial stance is uncommon in Swiss politics and business. Dr Marcel Trachsel, Managing Partner with the company 'int-ext communications' has lived in Canada and explains that Switzerland does not have a debating culture like those of Canada, the USA or Britain:

The Swiss are champions of compromise. The Swiss way to have an argument is for A to say red and B to answer with green. Then A keeps quiet. They will not negotiate it. One idea or the other will be chosen, or a compromise will later be found, depending on the vote of the others or on the influence of the 'opinion leader' in the group, whoever has the power. Even when there is a *Stammtisch* discussion (among the regulars at their favourite table in the local restaurant), it is done by everyone throwing out ideas and opinions, more as a kind of brainstorming than a debate. One of the reasons for avoiding criticising another person's ideas is that when criticism is made in Switzerland there is no custom of 'face-saving', or softening the negatives with positive comments. It tends to be pretty direct and hard-hitting. Those who live or work together prefer to avoid this, and say nothing. People will notice anyway when others don't agree.

The sanding-down process

A brochure for a museum exhibition on taboos[40] describes how Swiss cartoonists were asked, 'Do you have scissors in your head?' (*Schere im Kopf*) meaning, 'Do you edit taboo topics out of your cartoons?' My experience in writing this book was that Swiss people had sandpaper rather than scissors in their heads. I found I could quote my Swiss informants on anything they had said about their own country and people, but I often had to 'sand down' their comments afterwards to give them less of a rough edge. If X had said, 'It is absolutely impossible', when she later saw it in writing, she wanted it modified to 'It normally isn't possible'. People frequently made the comment, 'That's too black and white' about something they themselves had said earlier on tape. Many of my own comments were too provocative, or black and white and some were sanded down accordingly.

I realised that I had been raised in a culture of debate (and in fact took part in my first school debate when I was twelve) where you say things provocatively in public to distinguish your ideas clearly from the others and get the discussion going. The British political parties often disagree with each other in principle. Therefore, if the Tories say 'black', Labour is obliged to say 'white'. In Switzerland, when you are trying to achieve consensus, it is better to say 'light grey' versus 'dark grey' versus 'bluish grey' than 'white' versus 'black' versus 'blue'.

Consensus may mean it takes a long time to reach decisions. Charlie is from South Africa and has worked for ten years as a marketing manager for a medium-sized German Swiss company. Most of the staff are Swiss although many have studied and worked abroad. He describes typical decision-making processes in his work environment:

> A typical feature is 'democracy to the end', where everyone votes on everything. If two new people join a team in its second meeting, they need to have their say. However, there are very few dominant people, or strong characters who will push a decision through. For project work we hire external moderators to speed things up a bit. They can step on people's toes and do not have to be liked. The few dominant Swiss managers who exist can have a great career but they still need to have consensus behind them to carry out their goals. If a manager is too strong, people will do everything to go against him behind his back.

Unspoken decisions

Because Swiss people prefer to avoid conflicts, a consensus-based decision can take place very quietly. If newcomers are not paying attention, they may not notice anything has happened. They might think an issue has only been discussed, and opinions aired, but no decision was made, only to find at the next meeting that everyone else seems to know which decision was taken. The Swiss staff and tuned-in foreigners sensed which way things would go, but to avoid confrontation the decision was not stated clearly.

Consensus does not always mean everyone has to say their piece. Sometimes people are happy to go along with an 'opinion leader' who speaks for many. Once this person has spoken, the issue is also clear for silent group members who either had no strong opinions about it, or who are not willing to oppose this powerful person. It is important for newcomers to work out who the opinion leaders are. According to Rolf, a German Swiss manager in a large Swiss-based international company, it is normal to make a decision which pleases management, whether or not there is a debating culture:

> The group often feels or even knows who the opinion leader among them is, and may even try to find a solution which will please an outside influential person. I think this mechanism also applies to more argumentative groups. They would not provoke the mighty ones either. In our workplace we have consensus-driven decision making to some extent. I remember two young superiors of foreign origin who tried to introduce a strongly argumentative approach. In both cases this was felt to be unacceptable, and both of them eventually had to leave the company.

Ask specific questions

In meetings where there are many foreigners involved, this type of implicit, unspoken decision-making occurs less frequently. German staff are likely to influence the style of decision-making by giving their feedback as to what they think has happened, e.g. 'So as I understand it, we haven't decided yet whether the product will be red or green. Is that right? Will we decide at the next meeting?' Then the decision process is made more explicit.

Informal networking

For Germans in particular, with their more open, confronta-
tional debating style, conflict avoidance as a driving force in meetings can be very frustrating. If there is no clear statement of a decision, there can be no argument about it. An alternative approach
to asking specific questions (see box on previous page) is to find
out what is going on behind the scenes. Charlie, the South African
mentioned before, believes the best way to stay informed is by networking:

> While Germans express themselves better and come to the
> point more quickly, the Swiss are often self-conscious about
> speaking out. They may feel inhibited about their 'poor' High
> German or their 'poor' English. To compensate they sometimes
> form packs. If you are a foreigner, informal networking, (rather
> than open conflict) is crucial to find out what is going on, and who
> is with you or not. You need an undercover network to prepare you
> for meetings, so that you know others' positions. This does not
> mean friendship but rather a good cordial relationship. Having
> lunch together is an ideal way to keep abreast.

German Swiss staff do not usually meet at the bar after work.
They tend to keep their private lives strictly separate. Charlie suggests lunch as the best time for a chat, and coffee breaks are another opportunity to keep up to date informally. Marcel Trachsel
also points out that it is a disadvantage if Anglo-American staff
have a sandwich at their desks for lunch, because they then miss a
key opportunity to talk about work.

Ariane reports: Joining a company or a department in the French part of Switzerland is often like becoming part of a family, and rituals to build up informal exchanges are many. You are expected to join in. I joined an organization in Geneva, and was working for a dominantly French / French Swiss department. Eager to leave the office for a well-deserved weekend on Fridays, I didn't join the ritual apero (drink) on Fridays at 5.30 pm for a few months until the secretary asked me if I had read the small print in my contract. . .

Another ritual of this kind in Geneva was the daily common coffee break in the morning, and the one weekly morning meeting with croissants for everybody. Furthermore, many sub-departments were having lunch together every single day, and some had drinks together at the end of the day once or twice a week. It wasn't unusual to have real family links created between the workers, colleagues being made godfathers to each other's children etc.

The significance of coffee breaks

In Swiss departments across the country where there is no strong Anglo influence, the coffee break is a ritual event at a set time. No matter how busy staff are, they get together for it. A British employee in a Zurich-based company told me he preferred to take his coffee to his desk because he didn't understand the Swiss German spoken in the coffee room. It is quite likely that not understanding Swiss German dialect can cause people to miss some of the important, if informal comments in which people are revealing their allegiances in the company's internal politics. Swiss German speakers consider High German a foreign language. They are always willing to speak High German to foreigners, but find it unnatural to keep it up in all their conversations with each other. It is worth learning to understand Swiss German too.

Decisions made in advance

In Charlie's predominantly Swiss company, when foreigners were present, Swiss staff formed packs, or cliques in order to find out the opinions of other Swiss as to what was going on. In an international company there are potentially many variations on how decisions are reached, depending on numerous factors which could fill a book by themselves. An interesting case is the comparison made by André, who worked in a Swiss-led team of Swiss and Germans in an international company, and then after some restructuring, the group had English management.

In the Swiss-led meetings held in German we rarely had very strong personalities. You had to have agreement with your peer group and that involved large amounts of discussion. The boss tended to be steering but relying on the group to come to the right approach. People were generally fairly open about their opinions, saying 'I believe this' and giving a rationale. They didn't necessarily reach agreement straight away, but over the course of time they would negotiate, find a middle road and might have to call another meeting. The new English bosses now run meetings where everything has been discussed ahead of time on a one-to-one basis and then they go into the meetings to formalise things. This new way is starting to permeate though the whole company. Some guy wants a decision made in some way, and rather than coming cold into the meeting, he's done a lot of networking beforehand, much more than I would have anticipated. The general strategy has already been agreed on. The meeting is held to optimise it, stamp agreement and move on. This way you miss out on all the potential disagreements in meetings. I'm neutral about whether it is more efficient or not. More people tend to be involved in meetings than in the past, just to make sure everyone's agreeing.

This case is not a model of a typical English meeting style in a Swiss environment. Rather, it is an interesting example of the way one particular group of English managers started to handle meetings when they came to work at the headquarters of a particular Swiss-based company. It is significant that the new way did not cause open conflict. That would have been the least acceptable way to go in a Swiss setting.

Consensus and power

Paolo is Ticinese and describes how hierarchical thinking can be combined with the 'power of the people' in decision-making in the local community:

> Even when you have committee meetings to discuss a matter, it is the Latin expectation that the final decision will be passed back up to 'the people that count', for example the politicians, who often come from influential local families. But they often don't have much idea about the matter under discussion. If people want, they can have more responsibility. They sometimes influence the decision by spreading it around the community that the people want A, not B. The powers-that-be hear this and then choose A.

Chapter 18   Understatement

Self-promotion

It was mentioned previously that Swiss people do not praise others much at work because it is taken for granted that they will be doing a good job. They also prefer not to praise themselves. This is one of the reasons that it is hardly noticed abroad when Switzerland spends money on humanitarian efforts around the world. The Swiss believe their work will speak for itself. Back home companies and individuals tend not to sell themselves either and there is a wariness of over-enthusiastic company statements. Christoph Meier, Press Officer for UBS Bank in Zurich has also worked in the USA and finds the PR style in the two countries very different.

The US way of making a statement involves expressing emotion. There you say, 'We're really excited about this new project'. The Swiss wouldn't believe that. It is better to use understatement here. In the USA your company can give a donation to charity and really publicise it. For Swiss companies it loses its effect if they refer to it too much. They should only briefly mention it. US directors will also mention charity work on their CVs. Swiss directors will only write about their professional commitments.

The charity work of a high-level Swiss director might already be known among his Swiss peers even if he doesn't mention it. This cannot be assumed in the USA.

No need to boast

When I was helping Walter Dettling, Professor at the University of Applied Sciences in Basel, to prepare a short biography (or CV) for an American readership, I had to persuade him to briefly mention an innovative book he had co-authored on e-commerce.[41] I later compared his finished biographical details with the short biography of an American peer with a similar profile. The American biography said, 'B holds the distinction of co-authoring several best-selling books on x, y and z'. Wendy, an English teacher from England, comments that in Britain, like the USA, your CV is a document to help you sell yourself, while in Switzerland it is more a list of what you have done.

In Switzerland there is often less need to spell out all your activities because people know you. Professor Dettling is the president of Ecademy, recognised by the government as the National Centre of Competence for E-Business and E-Government. It can be assumed that anyone who is knowledgeable about the subject of e-commerce in Switzerland will be familiar with his publications too.

Not competitive

Beat is Swiss and married to Debby from the USA. They have lived in both the USA and Switzerland with their two children.

Debby believes that in Switzerland no one should excel because others will be envious. Beat finds that in general schools and their pupils are not as competitive in Switzerland as in the USA:

> In Switzerland no one says, 'We want to be the best'. A person with a competitive attitude is not liked. In the USA you hear it every day, 'We have the best school' etc. Individuals and schools think 'We can do anything if we want to, even be the world's best'. In Switzerland we are modest in general and don't say we are the best. This tends to hold the better students back a bit.

With regard to talking about personal performance, Switzerland is changing, at least in international companies. Swiss and British staff who have worked in Switzerland for a long time report that nowadays you need to keep selling yourself constantly and pedal hard in order to stay in the same place. If you do not communicate clearly from day to day what you are achieving, someone else will be promoted before you. A Swiss manager commented that Swiss staff are unlikely to say, 'I can do a,b,c really well', even if they can. English speakers sell themselves better, and good Swiss staff may be overlooked.

I'm not so important

Staff in small and medium-sized Swiss companies are not under the same pressure. They can be modest and others interpret it positively. I once gave an in-company workshop in which we were discussing a controversial decision which the small company had to make. One participant said, 'I am not so important in the company. This issue has to be decided by others'. A member of the board of directors was also participating and he answered, 'You're the head of the Task Force. That's a key function.' People cannot afford to talk so modestly in the Anglo-influenced competitive climate of the international companies.

Status symbols: my mineral water is lukewarm

In Switzerland small is beautiful, and power is played down. People are not usually ostentatious. At the root of this lies the belief that no one should stand out (see also chapter 14 on taking up space). There has never been the pomp and ceremony of an emperor or royal family and aristocracy at the head of the country. This can also affect the value placed on status symbols. It may not only be because the country is environment-conscious that many managers are not given a company car.

> Erik, an Englishman who worked for 11 years in Switzerland commented: What I liked most about Swiss people was the charming and disarming way they have for bringing 'big shots' down to earth. I guess that this quality has played a major role in their highly successful democracy.

Klaus, a German manager working for a Swiss pharmaceutical company in its German affiliate was promoted to the company headquarters in Basel. I asked him what he found most different about Basel. He said with great feeling, 'I am not allowed a fridge in my office. I have to buy lukewarm mineral water from the cafeteria'. What he found strange was that there were variations from building to building as to whether staff were allowed to have their own fridges and coffee machines, but these were not directly related to the seniority of the staff. Seniority did not seem to make certain privileges automatic.

Carlo, a Spanish manager who had been promoted from Spain to his company's Swiss headquarters said it was a bit of a let down that managers were not made to feel they were important at headquarters. He was surprised that they had so little assistance from secretaries. If he was organising a Saturday meeting for doctors in Zurich, he had to do everything himself, even organise the drinks.

Looking after yourself

The above examples show different attitudes towards status symbols within the same company in different countries. However, foreign staff who have worked in Switzerland for 10 or even 20 years will get used to Swiss ways and may be surprised by the expectations of their fellow countrymen. When there was an influx of English-speaking management to the Swiss headquarters of a large company, the English-speaking staff who had been there a while were surprised about the importance the new Anglo bosses attached to status symbols. High level managers needed bigger offices with bigger desks than local staff at the same level, and also needed a secretary to arrange their meetings for them, while Swiss, German and Anglo bosses (who had been in Switzerland a while and had 'gone local') normally arranged their own meetings. They considered it a technical matter, involving fairly easy technology which you could programme the computer to arrange. For the incoming bosses it was a matter of status.

At a lower level, new Anglo managers found themselves attending to many administrative details, like finding out flight times, which their personal assistants had taken off their hands back home. Swiss secretaries expected managers to 'look after themselves' to a greater degree than the Anglo managers had previously experienced. The exact role of secretaries is an issue no one thinks of discussing (or has time to discuss) when internal reorganisation is taking place and staff are being transferred abroad. It then comes as a surprise when there is a difference in expectations.

Chapter 19   Business etiquette

Swiss etiquette books for business people tell you basic things like not tucking your serviette into your collar at lunch and not talking with your mouth full. The focus in this chapter is not on these points, but rather on Swiss etiquette which may vary from that of English-speaking cultures. If you are working in a very international environment, there will obviously be variations, but even international companies tend to have pockets of mainly Swiss management, especially near the top!

Some of the tips mentioned below have already been discussed elsewhere but are summarised here from a business perspective, for people who will only dip into the business section of the book. If you are reading the book from cover to cover, you will read similar points again, from a slightly different angle.

Etiquette for daily business

Greetings: If you haven't skipped the first half of the book, you will know by now that greetings matter. In the business context, it is very important to greet colleagues you know when you arrive at work in the morning. It is also appreciated if you say hello to fellow employees in corridors and lifts, even if you have never been introduced. If you are leaving just before midday, you may find people wish you a nice lunch (*en guete*), and at the end of the day people tend to wish each other a nice evening. These are optional but are little gestures which help create a good atmosphere.

E-mail: Cultural issues are also issues online. Always greet your virtual colleagues as well as those you see face to face. Call the person by name at the beginning: 'Dear Hans', and use a suitable greeting at the end too, e.g. 'Regards, Sue', unless you are continuing the same conversation over the course of the day. It is a nice gesture to wish people a good day, evening, week, weekend, etc. in e-mail. (See also chapter 4 on correct behaviour and chapter 21 on use of first names and surnames).

From a study of 606 German language e-mails from Swiss banks, the researcher Ulla Kleinberger Günther[42] concluded that opening and closing greetings are obligatory in business e-mail. In private e-mail the writer's name at the end is the only obligatory part.

On the phone: German Swiss answer the phone by saying their surname. They often ask me in class why English speakers just say 'hello'. (I point out that this is also common practice in the Italian and French speaking parts of Switzerland). English speakers sometimes find saying the surname only is unfriendly, and if they say their names, they usually say both first names and surnames.

One reason Swiss people don't say both names is because this is how children are taught to answer the phone, to differentiate themselves from their parents. The other reason is that their first name is for use with their friends, and people who don't already know it don't really need to be told it.

Business attire: This is fairly relaxed, and many business people like to take every opportunity to dress casually. Most Europeans have never worn school uniforms and are not used to a uniform look (except in the army). They tend not to wear ties as much as English speakers (I know German and Swiss scientists who only wear ties on days they have meetings with senior management or clients). They often wear trousers and blazers in co-ordinated colours rather than a matching suit. English speakers can be overdressed by Swiss standards, and pinstripe suits are considered very 'Anglo'. Skirts no longer have any special significance for Swiss women. The right quality of trouser suit can be just as dressy.

Use of titles: Swiss people do not usually introduce themselves by their title, e.g. Doctor or Professor, as it would be considered boastful. Titles are used by others to introduce people to each other formally. Within companies, people tend not to address each other by their titles at all in day-to-day business. You will see people's titles along with their address after their signatures in their e-mails, and on formal documents. The exception is medical doctors, who are normally addressed as 'Herr Doktor' or 'Frau Doktor' by non-medical people.

Arriving at a business or social event

* First impressions matter. If others are doing it, greet everyone by name and shake hands. If you have forgotten someone's
name, say so before you start to shake hands, and then when they
tell you it again, shake hands and use it e.g. 'Hello Hans', or 'Hello
Mr Meier'. Try to remember the name, because you will be saying
it again when you shake hands to leave.

* Don't shake hands too firmly. Instead, to show your good
character, look people straight in the eye. In the German-speaking
part of Switzerland, unbroken eye contact is not intrusive, not
even with the opposite sex. It is a sign of honesty and confidence,
as all Swiss-based human resource managers know, and many foreign interviewees do not.

* If people are milling about chatting, it's best to introduce
yourself before you start talking to someone you don't know. If
you find this hinders spontaneity, say your opening sentence, then
introduce yourself properly once the person has responded to it. It
is more typical of English-speaking cultures to have a chat with
someone when you don't even know their name (see also chapters
1 and 2).

* The higher level employee or the client should decide
whether you will use first names. If you are on a similar level, the
older person decides. It used to be that a woman had to take the

initiative to suggest to a man that they change to first names (even if he was older), but this is apparently no longer necessary.

* Do not interrupt people in conversation, unless it is urgent. Stand around nearby and try to catch someone's eye. When you are talking to others, make sure you never interrupt them while they talk (interrupting is reserved for politicians on TV talk shows). Unlike in English-speaking countries, silent pauses are not a sign of communication breakdown, but of reflection.

* When it is time to go, take your leave of each person individually, with a handshake, name and eye contact again. If you have forgotten someone's name, ask for it, so you can say it as you shake hands. If there is a lot going on around you, it might not be noticed if you miss it out.

* Be liberal with passing on your regards to others via the person you are saying goodbye to, for example if you know Mr Meier's colleague, Mrs Kunz, but she is not at this particular gathering.

> Depending on the working environment, there may be many little customs to watch out for. Fabio is a German Swiss pilot who used to work in Switzerland and now works in Norway. He says there are differences in the attention paid to certain details.
>
> 'In Switzerland the crew all waited for each other after the flight, and walked back to the terminal building together. In Norway each crew member just walks off to the terminal when they are ready. No one waits for anyone else.

Food and drink[43]

Business entertaining is more likely to take place in a restaurant than in someone's home, and it is usually without your partner. If you are invited to someone's house, see also chapter 10 on entertaining.

* Before starting to eat, say *en guete*, or *bon appetit*.

* Wait till the host / hostess / boss says 'cheers' (*prost* or *santé*) before you start your wine. You can also say cheers with mineral water; it doesn't need to be alcohol.

> The most crass entertaining mistake made on the continent by English people is with wine, according to Siegfried, a German who describes a typical scene: 'At international business gatherings the wine has been poured, and the Germans and Swiss are sitting politely waiting to say 'cheers' as a group, while the English are already 'pouring it down'.'

* The traditional, hearty approach to toasts is to clink glasses with everyone present and say cheers individually to each one. For elegant occasions the etiquette experts recommend the following ritual: Holding the glass by the stem, everyone raises his or her glass to chin level and says 'cheers' to the whole group, looking all the others in the eye in turn, and tipping the glass in the direction of each. Then they all take a sip and give a little nod to the others before putting their glasses down. This seems to be a fashionable development in elevated circles in Switzerland (they don't

clink glasses in Paris after all). A rule of thumb with all these aspects of etiquette is to be observant and let the others take the lead.

* Having a drink may be an opportunity for someone (usually the more senior person or the older one) to suggest changing over to first names. The senior person says, 'I'm Hansruedi', even if you know this already, and you reply, 'I'm Charlotte', even although he knows that too, then you clink your glasses, both saying *Prost* and the other person's first name. Young Swiss staff often comment on the reluctance of older management to change to first names, ever.

* Although it is polite to wait until everyone is served, if it is a large group and slow service, people may insist that those who already have their food should start eating, rather than let the food get cold. If someone says this, they mean it (Swiss people are unlikely to say things they do not mean).

* People keep their hands on the table during the meal, rather than on their laps.

* Don't put your purse, handbag, mobile phone or keys on the table.

* Be prepared that people are going to smoke at the table. Offices are often non-smoking zones, but there is great public tolerance for cigarette smoke in restaurants. Smokers are still restaurants' best customers.

Ariane comments:

In the French part of Switzerland, an important ritual when going for lunch or dinner is to always have one female sitting next to a male at a table. It would be considered rude to have three men sitting next to each other, and three women sitting next to each other. This struck me, as the only French speaker, at a residential training course in Interlaken (in the German-speaking region). The first evening everybody rushed to the table, sitting just where they felt like, and nobody except me seemed to care who was sitting next to each other. After two years, this fact still makes me feel odd, and I still notice when four men are sitting next to each other, without females to enlighten their conversations - and vice versa.

Eye contact

Eye contact is one of the areas in which people do not question the rightness of what they do, perhaps because they learnt it at a very young age. Parents in western cultures say, 'Look at me when I'm talking to you' and in many non-western cultures they say, 'Don't look at me when I'm talking to you'. Frank is from South Africa and mostly speaks German to his colleagues in a Swiss company. He jokingly describes his experience of eye contact as 'eyeballing':

Eyeballing is the practice of making firm penetrating eye-to-eye contact when toasting with somebody at a drinks party or at the dinner table. This eye contact cannot just be broken when one of the parties wishes it, as a slight nod of the head is needed from both parties before taking your eyes away. In South Africa deep penetrating eye contact makes most people feel uncomfortable. I can clearly remember my father explaining to me as a child that fleeting eye contact is polite, but that one should never stare.

In German-speaking Switzerland maintaining eye contact as you speak is a sign of your integrity as well as your degree of confidence. When people avoid looking you in the eye, it can be interpreted that they have something to hide. Human resource managers describe this as a key factor in making a decision about a job candidate.

Doris is German Swiss and works for an executive recruitment company in Zurich. She works with colleagues who originate from Switzerland, Canada and Italy, and who all consider this point very important in their assessment centre exercises to recruit staff to work in Swiss companies.

Americans in particular look less into your eyes. Compared with them, English people look at you more directly, so I wonder if it is connected with a concern about sexual harassment on the part of the Americans. When people don't look at me directly, it gives me the impression they are not serious or not honest, although I know it is in fact a cultural difference. In the assessment centre I need to take it into consideration because even if it is okay for them, it may not come across well in the Swiss company they are interested in working for. In Sales and Marketing, for example, they will not 'get the deal' if they cannot maintain strong eye contact. If the candidate is otherwise suitable, I mention eye contact in my report as something to work on.

Firm eye contact can be misinterpreted by people from English-speaking cultures. If someone is cool and looks at you penetratingly, you may feel unnerved by it. If they behave warmly and also look deep into your eyes, you may start to get the wrong idea. It is a tricky issue.

To sensitise yourself to what different cultures consider a normal length of time to look into people's eyes, try zapping the remote control of your TV around 8.30 pm, to get a variety of TV channels from Switzerland and the surrounding countries. Compare what kind of eye contact people make in talk shows or documentary interviews. Although it is also a question of personality, Swiss German and German speakers are more likely to maintain unbroken eye contact with the other person throughout the interview, whether they are talking or listening, while Swiss French and Swiss Italian speakers may blink more, look away occasionally or look thoughtfully at the table or a wall, especially as they speak. Swiss German interviews are often conducted with people standing opposite each other to obtain maximum eye contact. In British talk shows, chairs are often placed almost side by side so that people are not constantly looking right at each other, but rather have to turn a bit to look.

Vivian is Swiss and told me that when she was at university she refused to attend the lectures given by an Austrian professor because he looked at the back wall while he was talking.

Chapter 20 Small talk

After an in-company workshop, I was having lunch with a
Swiss personnel manager, an English IT manager and a Swiss IT
consultant. I had met the personnel manager once before but did
not know the others at all. By far the most lively conversations
were about company issues, such as recent restructuring and
trends in knowledge management. We also chatted a bit about the
army, and cultural issues. The English IT man talked about his
family, giving an example of family dynamics while making a
point about cultural issues. It was noticeable that no one else re-
ciprocated with comments on *their* family dynamics. The subject
was probably a bit too private.

Some people in the German-speaking part of Switzerland really hate small-talk. It is referred to disparagingly as 'chatter'
(*Geschwätz*) and 'superficial conversation'.[44] The business
monthly magazine *Bilanz*[45] defined small-talk as 'non-committal'
(*unverbindliche*) social conversation, and even suggested it was
like a kind of role play (see illustration on the next page). The
Swiss business press regularly has articles trying to explain the
value of small-talk to unconvinced business people. For example,
the *Bilanz* article said '*Smalltalk* (as it is now called in German)

Non-commital social conversation by noyau

can result in an interesting conversation and lay a foundation for a deeper relationship'. The implications are that people think if nothing more meaningful results, then it has been a waste of time. In Switzerland there is a certain resistance to chatting to strangers as if they were friends, and it is considered intrusive to ask too many questions, although this is increasingly being recommended by Swiss communication trainers. The *Bilanz* article was entitled, *Fragen hilft weiter*, which means, 'It helps to ask'.

Taboo topics

Etiquette experts are often quoted as recommending discussion topics like holidays, hobbies and food. Politics, religion and money are all taboo. In the *Handelszeitung*[46] business newspaper, Mari Serrano reports the golden rule at company drinks parties is that people should not talk about work, their private problems, or others who are not present. With a touch of irony he says this leaves chatting about the cinema, sport, cars and your diet. Surprisingly, at the end of the article (written in autumn 2001), experts are quoted as saying catastrophes are suitable small-talk topics, as small-talk has an important function in comforting people.

Tennis or golf?

An American book on making conversation describes good conversation as like playing a game of catch:

> First one person has the conversational ball and talks, then after a bit tosses the conversation to the other person. This 'toss' can be in the form of a question, a request for an opinion, or a comment from the person whose turn it is to talk . . . By tossing the conversational ball back and forth, the participants can balance the input and output of information about one another.[47]

In Switzerland when people who do not know each other stand around chatting, I experience it more like a game of tennis. The speaker does not hold on to the ball long (talking about yourself at length is not always appreciated) but sends it back quite fast. In a course where participants were practising 'chatting', Petra commented that her partner was playing golf, not tennis. He didn't send questions back in her direction.

If someone is not responding much, he or she may not see the point of small-talk. Try bringing a third person into the conversation and as a last resort, move away from 'superficial' topics and ask about something serious, like company politics, or current affairs.

Work and current affairs

In choosing your conversation topics it may be helpful to ask, 'What would Swiss people actually *like* to be talking about, if there were no taboos?' At the lunch mentioned at the beginning of the chapter, conversation really got going when people exchanged ideas on company changes and trends. This is not talking shop in the way you would ask a colleague, 'What did you think of that proposal I sent you?' Talking or 'gossiping' about the workplace is the most interesting topic for many employees.

Another 'taboo' topic which may get people talking if handled well is Swiss current affairs. Matthias, a German Swiss manager commented that he finds it a pity that he cannot discuss Swiss issues with his colleagues because they are all foreign and do not know anything about Swiss politics.

Politics is a subject dear to many Swiss people's hearts. There are many evening talk shows on German Swiss TV, featuring people discussing political topics with great enthusiasm, like Switzerland's relationship with the rest of the world or the next *initiative* or referendum, of which there are several every year. Foreigners often comment on the in-depth understanding Swiss people have of politics, like Sharon from the USA, who herself has a strong interest in world politics:

> I am amazed about the degree of political awareness in Switzerland. When I talk to somebody here about politics, they understand what I am talking about and they can respond. There's a clarity, a sharpness about it, as people say, 'I've read something about this. Here are my thoughts about it'.

Christine is German and also finds Swiss people very well-informed on a wide range of topics:

People have a clear world view, and a definite opinion about everything, from politics to child-rearing. They never say, 'I have no idea'. I think it comes from the voting methods, where people have to say 'yes' and 'no' to all kinds of large and small issues. They have thought everything through.

Your Swiss colleagues may appreciate your showing an interest in Swiss current events. It will not turn into a controversial political debate if you take the approach of asking questions in order to understand the issue and the country better. Even if you have only read the headlines in a Swiss newspaper with a dictionary in your hand, you can ask Swiss colleagues to explain in more detail and give your their opinions so that you can become more informed. If you can speak German, you could dip into some of the articles in a weekly Swiss magazine like *Facts* or *Die Weltwoche*.

Chapter 21   The 'Du' virus

The frequently-mentioned issue of whether to use first names or surnames is a talking point for Swiss people as well as English speakers in Switzerland. Swiss society is changing, and social customs are changing with it, although there is some resistance to this. In a Swiss business newspaper, the *Handelszeitung*[48] Thomas Pfister writes a very funny article in which he uses the expression '*Du*-attacks' to describe people introducing themselves in the workplace by their first names.

Pfister portrays the *Du*-attack as an assault at the coffee machine or in the confines of the lift, where the opponent says, 'Hello, I'm Hans-Peter!' and extends a threatening hand in the direction of his colleague's stomach. Then there is the subtle approach at the office Christmas party. Every time you clink glasses, someone slips it in: 'By the way, my name is Toni'. The recipient of the 'offer' of intimacy is so taken aback, he just stammers his first name in response, and may even add weakly, 'pleased to meet you.'

Pfister puts this '*Du*-virus' down to globalisation. He points out that the custom of saying *Du* to colleagues has been around in Switzerland since the 1968 student movement, but that it was then the elite *Du* of a team, e.g. teachers, the police or journalists, who were distinguishing insiders from the outsiders. Now the *Du* form is losing its special significance as the form used by people working together regularly, or more closely. Staff who work in an international environment may use first names with everyone rather than just with their own team. In the French part of the country, using first names does not automatically mean saying *tu*.

> Ariane reports: Although perceived as less formal than the German Swiss, the French Swiss are at times much more formal when showing respect and acknowledging authority. There is a tendency to switch quickly to the informal *tu* with first names among colleagues. But a handy way to show respect and a certain familiarity at the same time, is to use the first name, followed by the formal *vous*.
>
> For more than 12 years, I had the least 'bossy' boss one can imagine. But while I used the informal Miriam, *tu* with his wife, I used the more respectful Alain, *vous*, with him throughout our common working years. Similarly, with many intercultural and consultant colleagues here in Geneva, we use the (informal) first name combined with the (formal) *vous*.

Using first names and *Sie* is also an option for Germans. German Swiss find this too illogical. It is a *halbe Sache*, or half measure. They also find it unacceptable if the respect goes one way only, for example that the boss should be 'Mr Smith' and the secretary 'Denise', or the lecturer, 'Professor Simpson' and the student, 'Andrew'. This is a traditional custom in English-speaking countries where surnames can be used to show respect for position, seniority or age. The custom is dying out except within the medical profession. British people who have lived in Switzerland are shocked to report that in hospitals in Britain the doctor calls the patient 'John' or 'Liz', but the patient is expected to say 'Dr Taylor' in return. In German-speaking Switzerland this would not be understood, as the doctor would then be expressing closeness while the patient was expressing distance.

> The *Hallo* virus?
> It was mentioned in chapter four that children learn to say *Grüezi* to adults in the street when they are learning *Anstand* (correct behaviour). It has however been my observation that children in the Basel area are increasingly saying *Hallo* to adults they know, instead of *Grüezi,* and are also saying *Hallo* to each other instead of S*ali*. I asked some nine-year-old children in Steingruben school in Riehen about this, and some told me they only say *Grüezi* to adults they know if they are actually shaking hands. Perhaps *Hallo* is also a 'virus' that will sweep the country, and blur the distinction between the different forms of address for adults and children.

Du in small companies

For people visiting or working in small Swiss companies it is worth noting again that names have a symbolic meaning for people who do not move in international circles. Traditionally, changing to first names implies a degree of closeness which can be as much a burden as a benefit in people's working lives. The degree of personal commitment they want may be a factor influencing whether they choose to be on first-name terms. Christian is a Swiss project manager who compares the custom in small Swiss companies and large international companies.

When I worked for a small Swiss company, I avoided going to certain dinners where I would be expected to have a drink and get on a first name basis with people. This would create a degree of intimacy more like in the family. This reluctance is a very Swiss mentality and a big issue in small companies, but which would not have the same meaning in large firms like Credit Suisse, ABB or IBM.

The washcloth

Markus Schneider, a political journalist reporting from the *Bundeshaus*, the Federal Parliament in Berne, wrote in the Swiss weekly *Facts*[42] magazine that it was important for him to avoid certain occasions with politicians, like outings involving alcohol, which might provide an opportunity for them to get on first name terms with him. Once they were on first name terms, he would become a 'wash cloth' (*Waschlappen*) or a softie, rather than a good journalist who reports impartially and asks the necessary awkward questions. He explained that he is just not firm enough with his *Duz-Freunde* (friends with whom he uses first names and says *Du*).

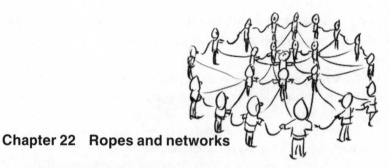

Chapter 22   Ropes and networks

The Englishman's home . . .

It has already been mentioned that German Swiss business people are unlikely to go for a drink after work but enjoy taking time to talk over lunch, which can last more than an hour. Some staff work in the same department for years without revealing details of their private lives to co-workers, and their co-workers respect their privacy. It is also more unusual for German Swiss staff to invite work colleagues to their homes for dinner than in highly mobile English-speaking circles where people often treat their colleagues as friends. In the French part of Switzerland, this may be a bit different.

Connecting ropes

Because German Swiss do not seem to socialise much with their co-workers outside the workplace, it can be a surprise to foreigners if long-term connections with people outside the company influence decision-making. This is reported more often by people who do not work in an international environment. People without

Ariane reports: In Geneva it is almost considered a duty of a boss to invite all his staff to his home once a year at least. One of my big bosses usually had a garden party for the division in the quiet holiday month of August (to avoid trying to squeeze everybody into his house). The boss of each department of the division did the same, too. Clients may be invited home, too, but not as frequently. You'd probably invite them out to a good restaurant to start with.

French Swiss, although less formal than German Swiss in a private setting, are very formal when being introduced to people with personal authority over them. And clients are considered as a kind of authority to start with. But since good relationships are the foundation of fruitful collaboration, emphasis can quickly be given to exchanging personal information in order to build up mutual trust.

Once every two months, a client from France visited Claudine in Geneva to develop tailor-made products. Quickly Claudine knew quite a bit about this French family firm, was invited to visit the production site in France, was introduced to the family, and also received the announcements for both the babies who happened to enlarge the family. Each working meeting started with an exchange of personal information just to see how things had evolved since the previous meeting. Throughout this working relationship, the familiar/respectful *vous* plus first name was kept.

good connections have less chance of influencing decisions. While it is common in English-speaking countries to talk about networking, German Swiss know both networks and *Seilschaften*.

Seilschaften is the word used for groups of people roped together in mountain climbing. Ropes have usually been tied years before, at school or university, in job training, or in the army, where people worked together and learned to trust each other. Marcel Trachsel comments that it does not have to mean they are good friends, but more that A is prepared to recommend B because he knows B does a good job. People in *Seilschaften* feel a sense of commitment to each other, and ropes can help them climb the career mountain.

Networking is different. It is newer, and the word is borrowed from English, unlike the traditional Germanic word, *Seilschaften*. Networking is on the increase in Switzerland as people become more mobile and move away from the area where their ropes were tied. When people network, they are often establishing new contacts. The net patterns can criss-cross in all directions, linking many people on quite a large scale. C will pass on D's name even if she doesn't know much about him. She is not necessarily vouching for his ability.

Chapter 23   Switzerland works

People I interviewed invariably commented on efficiency and stability as things they appreciate in Switzerland. Someone said "In Switzerland you can anticipate that what was true yesterday will be true tomorrow." Specifics mentioned were public transport, banking systems, punctuality and reliability, and quality of workmanship. People usually pay bills on time and obey the rules. Most of them buy tram and bus tickets even though there is rarely an inspector around to check whether they have their tickets. They separate their garbage into paper, cardboard, glass, aluminium, oil, batteries, etc., and dispose of it all appropriately and responsibly.

Working times

The time people start work also contributes to the image of Swiss efficiency. Marla, an English manager, reports her observations of her department in an international company:

> Most Swiss arrive between 6 am and 8 am, the French and Germans generally between 7.30 and 8.30am, and most Americans/

British/Irish between around 8 and 9.30 am. The Swiss tend to be
more involved in local clubs in their community in the evening so
they prefer to start earlier and still have a work-free evening. Foreigners start later and work later, or take work home.

If Swiss staff are very busy, they will probably start even earlier rather than work very late. Claudia, who is German Swiss, told
me her computer-specialist husband had so much work for a period that he had started taking the 5.28 am tram, and was in his office by 5.50. He then worked until 7 pm. Sometimes she joined
him on the early tram if she was also having a busy spell at the office, then they still had time for dinner together in the evening.

Ariane reports: When listening to the traffic information on the
radio in the morning, you will quickly notice that the business traffic jams take place later in the morning in the French part of Switzerland than in the German parts. French Swiss prefer to start to
work between 8 and 9 am, an hour after the German Swiss have
arrived at work. This even influences diary layout, as Annette, a
German Swiss who moved to Nyon, pointed out to me recently.
You won't find a French diary starting any earlier than 8 am,
whereas German ones may start at 7 am.

All this makes the Swiss sound rather energetic. According to
Demoscope, a Swiss research and marketing company, more than
half of the Swiss population begin the day full of *elan* or energy.[50]
These people are seldom tired, in contrast to only one sixth of the
population who regularly feel lethargic or even exhausted.

The right time for a meeting

Different working times have implications for working life, as Marcel Trachsel reports from his experience of international project team work:

> The major working differences between the UK and Switzer-land are that the Swiss work from 8 till 6 and the Brits from 9 till 8. If the UK guy tells the Swiss guy there will be a meeting at 7 pm the Swiss guy is annoyed and vice versa, if the Swiss guy tells the UK guy there will be a meeting at 8 am he isn't too pleased either. The time at which they are both functioning well in the office is perhaps between 9 and 6.

> Ariane reports: French Swiss also take longer lunch breaks, during which many business matters can be discussed. Conse-quently, they also work later in the afternoon / evening, and task force meetings can be scheduled at 6 pm.

The well-oiled machine

La Suisse n'existe pas (Switzerland doesn't exist) was a slogan used by Swiss exhibitors at a Spanish exhibition in 1990. The statement is based mainly on the belief that Switzerland is a *Willensnation*, a nation created by the will of the people, but that the nation has no uniform ethnic or religious identity. At best, Swiss people will say it is united by its railway, its army and its political system, a distinctive style of democracy in which people vote on all aspects of their society at national, regional and local village community levels (which is actually quite an achievement). The question of national identity was answered by Dr Albert Debrunner, a Swiss scholar, as follows:

> Switzerland works. The people don't care about being a nation. They are too busy keeping things running smoothly, the smoother the better. Both the right and left wing lads are proud that Swiss trains run on time. The 6.05 train from Basel will get them to Zurich at 7.08. Switzerland is like a big company run by clever management. The employees have a say in how the plant is run, and that is why it is still working. The management is the government, at both cantonal and federal level. The way we organise ourselves is positive and efficient, and we don't want this to change.

Albert Debrunner's comments remind me of the designation of Switzerland as a well-oiled machine, made by the Dutch interculturalist, Geert Hofstede.[51] Hofstede provides four models of company culture: the well-oiled machine, the village market, the pyramid of people and the family. These descriptions are a broad generalisation, and company cultures are obviously too complex for a comprehensive description in this book. However, people do recognise some basic truths in Hofstede's models.

Swiss companies, along with companies in Germany, Austria, Finland and Israel, are said to be well-oiled machines, running very efficiently. Clear procedures are in place, the rules resolve problems and there is limited dependence on bosses. There is a strong preference for more rules and regulations. Related to this is a working style by which you have to stick to plans and follow through on what you said you would do. Hofstede comments:

> The need for laws and rules is not based on formal logic but on psycho-logic . . . as little as possible should be left to chance.
> The emotional need for rules in strong uncertainty avoidance societies can be turned into a talent for precision and punctuality. This is especially the case where power distances are relatively small so that subordinates' behaviour does not depend on whether the boss looks or not.

In essence the well-oiled machine model requires structuring the activities without concentrating the authority. The rules, rather than a powerful leader, should settle all daily problems.

Ariane on efficiency: I was struck recently by how quickly people reply to e-mails in companies in the German-speaking part, even if just to confirm receipt. I sent out four e-mails to potential clients one day and had three replies within 24 hours. In the French part of Switzerland when I did the same thing, no one answered within a week.

A French Swiss, who's been living in the German part of Switzerland for a decade, recently commented on the German Swiss, "They stick to their deadlines, and are quick to reply. You need to be more patient when working with French Swiss".

The pyramid of people

The well-oiled machine contrasts with the company cultures of Latin countries and Japan, which Hofstede describes as a 'pyramid of people'. As Ariane describes, the company cultures of the French and Italian-speaking parts of Switzerland are also better described as pyramids of people (see Ariane's comments below). Formal, or 'official' rules are in place, but they may in practice not be obeyed. The role of the boss is therefore central, and the relationship network takes on importance in managing the system. There is a more hierarchical mentality in these cultures, which are known as 'high power distance' cultures.

Ariane on 'the pyramid of people': There are many fundamental differences between the different linguistic communities in Switzerland. This may reach the point that some German Swiss business people declare the Latin parts of Switzerland to be 'AGA' - *Alles Ganz Anders* or 'Everything Completely Different'. Why is this, and how do these differences manifest themselves more precisely?

The company culture type most often referred to for Switzerland is the 'well-oiled machine', where clear procedures are in place, and the dependence on the boss is limited. The 'pyramid of people' model, with more centralized power, strong personal relationships and social roles, rather than task-based roles, is more in tune with the Latin (French and Italian) cultures in Switzerland. Both the well-oiled machine and the pyramid of power can exist within one Swiss company, influenced by the cultures of the different heads of departments.

Ariane gives an example of the 'pyramid of people': Claudine worked in an international organisation based in Switzerland. She was a member of the department in charge of developing operational strategies and policies, which was led by a French Swiss, who most people addressed with a respectful 'Roland, *vous . . .* ' All the members of the department, the 'family', were received as a group every afternoon in his office to exchange the latest news and elaborate on some ideas, although all decisions were taken by him personally, or in one-to-one meetings only. All the staff, except one, was composed of native French speakers, and the most important team ritual was the apero late Friday afternoon, which is where they preferred to have an informal discussion.

The Logistics department, led by Adrian, a German Swiss, was on the same floor. This was a well-structured department, where the morning meeting served the purpose of allocating urgent duties and discussing problems or pending issues. Efficiency was the common goal that built up the team spirit. Once a year, the procedures and guidelines were up-dated, and the German and German Swiss staff made sure they were kept within the company.

In these cases, the 'department cultures' were clearly shaped by the cultural preferences of their leaders and their staff. Coincidentally, (or not?) the management styles served the purpose of the respective departments quite well, although tensions between them were frequent, with the two mentalities and cultures clashing regularly.

Village markets

Another contrast with the well-oiled machine is Hofstede's description of Dutch, Scandinavian and most western English-speaking cultures, which are known as 'village markets'. They tend to be similar to the well-oiled machine in their limited dependence on bosses. They generally differ from the well-oiled machine in that they have a higher tolerance of the unknown and their activity is determined by the demands of the situation rather than the rules. 'If frost ruins the tomatoes, we'll sell something else. And if they don't want tomatoes any more, we'll grow something else'. Flexibility is built into the system, short-term thinking prevails, and problems tend to be resolved ad hoc. A reasonable degree of uncertainty is okay and will be managed as part of the job.

> Village market cultures are more suited to retailing, e-commerce, information technology or investment banking, where supply and demand changes from week to week. In contrast, well-oiled machines are suited to the long-term planning required in bringing a product through the stages from invention to market in the engineering and pharmaceutical industries (Anyone who has compared trying to buy a replacement part for a washing machine in both Britain and Switzerland will understand the difference in short and long-term thinking here.

Although large international companies in German-speaking Switzerland often have staff of 50-60 different nationalities, the well-oiled machine model appears to dominate, while the Anglo-

American style village market seems to be gaining ground. Put simply, the smaller scale village market model is nested within the larger well-oiled machine, allowing for plenty of blurring at the edges between them. There are also myriads of sub-cultures within these main structures, like departmental cultures.

In international companies in German-speaking Switzerland, the traditional finance, supply chain (logistics) and production departments tend to function according to the well-oiled machine model, and are usually led by Swiss and German managers. They have a semi-permanent hierarchical structure and think more long-term, working according to clearly-laid down and well-refined procedures. The marketing and development departments tend to have more foreign staff and are increasingly being run along the lines of the flexible village market model. In the pharmaceutical industry, for example, there are few Swiss managers in high positions in marketing.

Chapter 24   Leadership

In an avalanche no snowflake feels responsible for the result-ing damage. (Elisabeth Gehrer, Minister of Education, Science and Culture, Austria[52])

One of the amazing features of the well-oiled machine is the ability of staff to keep working when there is no supervision. I re-member being impressed at how my clients from the logistics de-partment of a Swiss company continued to function conscien-tiously and effectively for six months on end after both the head of department and their group leader had left and had not been re-placed. Although people were unhappy about the situation, the work got done.

At higher levels, supervision may also be minimal if a boss has his or her office in another building, another town or even another country, and only visits the team every one to two weeks. There is regular e-mail contact, and continual on-site supervision is not expected. These are not typical scenarios, but I come across them from time to time. Having no boss on site is more likely to cause problems in a pyramid of people culture.

Ariane reports: French Swiss have a fundamental respect for personal authority. Much more than in the German-speaking parts of Switzerland, the boss here is still the boss, and staff are anxious not to make any decisions on their own:

Laurence, a French consultant who's been living in Germany and works in the German-speaking part of Switzerland, just started to work on a project with a number of Swiss associations. After a first three-day seminar she stated, "I was stunned to see the behaviour of the French Swiss. They kept on referring to their absent bosses, and didn't dare take any responsibility by themselves."

Leaders and schools

This contrast between the nature of leadership in the well-oiled machine and the pyramid of people can be seen clearly in Swiss state schools. The following comment comes from an official Swiss website in English on schooling:[53]

In general there are no head teachers as such in the German-speaking part of Switzerland at compulsory school level; if there are any, their tasks do not go beyond organisation and co-ordination. The set-up is slightly different, however, in the French-speaking part, where the head teacher's role is much more important (supervision and pedagogical responsibilities). At the upper secondary level, however, the position of head teacher is important throughout the country because there are no inspectors for schools which teach for school-leaving certificates.

(The 'school leaving certificate' refers to the *Matura*, the certificate which is required for university entrance.)

In schools in the German-speaking part, if there is a problem with a class or a teacher, there may be no 'management' on site with whom the parents can discuss the matter. In a town there may be a head teacher with responsibility for several schools, and in a village, the school board (consisting of local people) will be consulted. There is a trend to introduce on-site school management, but professional management is not a popular concept in some educational circles and many people prefer to keep the school the responsibility of lay people, e.g. the school board. They do not want head teachers providing strong leadership.

Leaders in politics

After the September 11th attacks on the USA in 2001, when CNN reported President Bush making a statement that America was at war, the TV cameras showed only Bush himself as he spoke. The Swiss TV cameras went round the whole room, showing all the people who were involved with him in the talks. CNN reported the views of a leader, while the Swiss reported the views of a group, summarised by their leader.

Who is right? If things go wrong in the USA at the federal level, the President is usually held accountable, and is penalised at the latest at the next elections. If things go wrong in Switzerland at this level, it will be the fault of no one person. There is a group of seven equal-ranking people in the Federal Council. They are in charge of the country, and each year a different council member is president. The group of seven are chosen from four different political parties from the right and the left, but they are all known for their moderate views within their own parties so that the council can more easily reach consensus.

A historical perspective on the effects of consensus is provided by Urs Späti:

> The degree of success of the Swiss political system in comparison with others in Europe can only be assessed over the centuries. In the Swiss system not much can go wrong but not much happens either. In history, Swiss failure was usually due to the inability to reach consensus and/or to being too slow. In political systems which allow for the consolidation of power (whether driven by kings, dictators or parliamentary democracies), good decisions can produce quantum leaps of progress whereas bad decisions can lead to great failures. In these systems there are just bigger degrees of trial and error on the way to sustainable progress.

Making mistakes

In a thought-provoking letter in the Swiss magazine *Das Magazin*,[54] Klaus Stohlker, a Swiss PR professional, describes a Swiss fear of making mistakes because someone who makes a mistake and is caught will be reminded of it all his life. It used to be that nothing changed for years on end in Swiss politics, industry and culture, and therefore every mistake kept its importance.

Leaders in industry

The ultra-democratic process of decision-making by consensus is also a key factor influencing business leadership profiles. The Swiss political landscape trains people to be champions in compromising and in finding an acceptable common denominator (see chapter 17). Marcel Trachsel comments that this can be seen as a strength or a weakness but it does not necessarily create great leaders.

Many Swiss companies also have an aversion to strong leaders and see the whole group as important. As Charlie, a South African manager, said, "The few dominant Swiss managers who exist can have a great career but they still need to have consensus behind them to carry out their goals." He believes that if a manager is too strong, people will do everything to go against him behind his back.

Charisma not wanted

The emphasis on consensus means that charismatic industry leaders are looked on with a certain degree of scepticism in German-speaking Switzerland. Statements by management experts go so far as to warn of the dangers of charismatic leadership. Professor Christoph Baitsch[55] told the *Basler Zeitung* newspaper:

> I consider it a very problematic development that . . . leaders must have charisma in order to exercise successful leadership. This suggests that someone wishes to inspire others on the basis

of personality characteristics, and that they will then follow blindly like sheep. This is not only dangerous, but it also has nothing to do with the modern science of leadership.

What are the qualities most appreciated in a German Swiss leader? In the weekly finance newspaper, *Cash*, David Bosshard generalised about the types of leaders most commonly found in Switzerland:[56]

* Harvard Engineers are the most dominant manager type in Switzerland, but are supposedly on the way out. They are described as fast moving technocrats with an MBA, who speed up processes, delegate and outsource, but are viewed by staff as not really possessing any authority.

* The Hyperpragmatist has a future at the top in Switzerland. He is slower than the Harvard Engineer and does not develop new strategies. His strength lies in implementing and optimising the achievements of his predecessor. In a crisis, he will become even more pragmatic than he is already. If this reminds you of a chartered accountant, you may not be far wrong. Finance specialists are often in the top positions in industry.

* Pioneers are particularly needed in start-ups. They have a lot of potential but 'little proof of sustained success'.

* Patriarchs and Leaders are not really welcome in the larger companies because of their authoritarian style, although

they are often found in small family-run companies. Bosshart believes that if they are too charismatic they come across as ridiculous.

There used to be quite a tradition of authoritarian leadership in Switzerland, and company heads were often also high-ranking officers in the army. Marcel Oertig, head of Human Resources at Swisscom Fixnet, Switzerland's main telecoms provider, believes that nowadays people are not impressed with authority for its own sake:

> There is less of the hierarchical 'Herr Direktor'-giving-orders style of management. Managers have a co-operative leadership style, involving more participation from staff. You see this in appraisals. Feedback is not only top-down, but also bottom-up, with staff being invited to comment on the performance of their superior.

Authoritarian leadership has not completely died out in large companies. After the merger between two German Swiss companies, A and B, people were surprised by the differences in company cultures.

Gottfried, a new employee who had to liase extensively with a wide variety of departments, reported that he could tell whether staff were ex-A or ex-B by the way they dealt with his enquiries. If he asked for some information and they just gave it to him, they were ex-A. If they said they would have to ask their boss first, they were ex-B.

Ariane reports: French Swiss leaders tend to assume a certain 'father' role in their leadership style. A high degree of respect for their authority is expected by the *patron* (or boss) and they are not too keen on flat hierarchies. But at the same time, they often show parental-type care towards their subordinates, and therefore can't generally be accused of authoritarianism.

In the Latin parts of Switzerland, many still feel more drawn to relationship-based working environments and hierarchies, rather than to working according to objectives or to fulfilling some tasks. Ideally, the French Swiss company's organigram should show the individual person, rather than describing the function. And at times, job descriptions are still tailor-made for the person in charge of the function, and not the other way round.

Joanne, an American married to a Swiss, could hardly believe it when she started working in Geneva. "Here, each time a person changes department, the whole set-up and routine of the department changes as well to fit the strength and personality of the newcomer. With clearly-defined job-descriptions, this couldn't happen, since the new person would have to fit into the given system, and not the other way round."

The pyramid of people also produces hierarchical management styles that can be a surprise to outsiders used to more egalitarian styles. Sylvia, a Swedish scientist, had been working on a two-year contract in an international organisation with a French Swiss as direct boss. People were happy with her work, and she naturally expected her contract to be extended. But to her great surprise, the human resources department suddenly informed her that the French Swiss boss had cancelled her job. Coming from a country where bosses were not such powerful figures, the fact that this decision had not been discussed previously with her was almost more shocking than her losing her job.

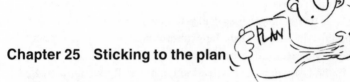

Chapter 25   Sticking to the plan

When we first got married, my husband wanted to show me some of the beauty of Switzerland. However, we had a bit of trouble planning our weekend excursions. I wanted to decide on Wednesday where we were going on Saturday, for example, to Grindelwald, but he didn't seem to want to commit himself to anything at all before Friday evening.

With time I realised that he did not want to agree to a plan because then things would be fixed, and as he saw it, he couldn't change his mind any more. And on Wednesday he didn't have all the information he needed to make the right decision about Saturday. What if we were very tired by Friday evening, or the weather turned out to be bad, or it was going to be better weather in another part of the country? As far as I was concerned, it didn't matter whether we really carried out our plan. Only the two of us were involved. We could change our minds every day from Wednesday to Saturday if we wanted, and finalise the plan or cancel the whole thing on Saturday morning if we were too tired.

Later, in the business world, I came across a similar phenomenon. Associated with the well-oiled machine model is the idea that things will go as planned. It is a typical German Swiss characteristic to be reliable and do what you have said you will do. When something has been decided it is assumed to be definite. 'Flexibility' can be a bit suspect in comparison. I often experience this in cross-cultural training seminars. I design and refine my course model according to the needs expressed by the course participants when I telephone them. They are happy to have a tailored programme, but when other issues come up during training, and I continue to refine my material from day to day, they get a bit frustrated. They are then faced with a flood of new handouts, 'hot off the press' which they have to find place for in the well-ordered binders I provide them with. My 'village market' supply and demand flexibility can get a bit much for them. In the written feedback someone once suggested I should hand out the FULL binder before the start of the course.

Unreliable foreigners?

As said in chapter 17, many international companies in Switzerland have employees from 50 or 60 different countries. This chapter focuses on typical misunderstandings reported in the communication between well-oiled machines (reliable) and village market (flexible) cultures. A standard problem is that reported by Peter, a Swiss project manager for a large international company. He regarded his US colleagues as unreliable:

> I was responsible for a big project to develop new global procedures, and I found it difficult to get our staff in the USA to do things as agreed. They would agree to all kinds of things in meetings, but then they wouldn't follow through. There seemed to be misunderstandings as to what exactly was agreed on.

Peter's comment is often made by German Swiss, and not only with regard to Americans. One German Swiss supply chain manager went as far as to say, "The staff in our foreign subsidiaries are a bit unreliable, except the Southern Germans." In industry it is the most frequent complaint about staff in other countries, and is caused to a certain extent by a difference in communication style.

Company politics

One explanation for the Americans not doing what they 'promised' could be that there was a power struggle going on between Peter's headquarters in Switzerland and the strong American subsidiary. This is common. In companies around the world people working at headquarters assume they have more authority, and try to implement global standards or a global marketing strategy. Meanwhile the subsidiaries have their own opinion as to what they need. In the case above, Switzerland was the headquarters, but the Americans had the biggest markets. The stage was set for a power struggle. It is not my intention to discuss the rights and wrongs of internal politics here, but rather to point out that power struggles and other political behaviour take place in a context and are handled differently according to the culture.

German Swiss staff behaving politically are not given to making promises they do not keep. They are more likely to look cautious and would perhaps claim they were not yet able to come to a decision for action at all. *Wir überprüfen es noch* (we're still checking it out) is a common excuse for inaction. People waiting for an answer are often heard to complain 'they're playing their cards close to their chest' when they can't work out what is going on. German Swiss staff are not likely to make a decision 'provisionally', then take it back again later.

The future as a fact

Another reason for misunderstandings as to what was agreed is that German Swiss believe in the importance of doing exactly what they have said. Any extenuating circumstances should be taken into account at the time of 'promising' so that they do not later have to change the plan. It is no coincidence that English has six future forms compared with only two in Swiss German.[57] To native speakers of English these six forms express different shades of meaning, including how likely it is that the person will do what they say. If someone is waiting for action, the comment: 'We will be implementing this plan next week' sounds more fixed and reassuring than 'we will implement this plan next week'. The second statement might be interpreted as just 'good intentions' in a flexible working environment.

In Swiss German there is a strong preference for using the present tense only to describe the future, as in 'we discuss it next week'. In English grammar this is the use of the 'future as a fact', like when we say, 'the train arrives at 10.15'. 'The future as a fact' is the most impersonal form, assuming there will be no personal factors or other influences which will cause a change of plan. The tense used seems to fit in English too. This does not mean German-speaking Swiss are naïve enough to think life is completely predictable but rather that they take other factors into account in the early stages when promising to do something, like my husband taking into consideration the weather in Grindelwald. If they do not have all the information, they will not commit themselves. At most they will say 'we might implement the plan next week'.

Express caution

When you are talking to German Swiss, it is a good idea to express caution and signpost the fact that you are not promising anything. Say, 'We'll try to get this up and running'. Do not say 'We will get this up and running soon' in order to sound positive and optimistic. To a German speaker, that is a promise. When dealing with English speakers, German Swiss need to practise active listening, i.e. listen quite carefully and check what seems to have been agreed, e.g. 'As I understand it, this system will definitely be in operation by the end of the month. Is that right?' or ask an open question, such as, 'How long will it take at most to get this up and running?'

Building trust

German Swiss network effectively on their home turf, and often comment on what helpful information they can pick up from colleagues over lunch or coffee. One of the challenges of business communication in international companies is that people are working regularly with colleagues in another country, communicating almost exclusively by telephone and e-mail, with the occasional video conference. They have little opportunity to actually see their business partners and pick up helpful information over coffee or lunch. Then it is a challenge to build up a clear picture of what's really going on in their partner's world.

In any situation where there are communication problems, no matter what culture you are dealing with, it can be assumed that e-mail contact alone is unlikely to solve them. The ideal is to find an opportunity to meet, socialise and get to know your business partners better. If you can schedule time for relaxing over meals into business trips, you can get a different perspective on their problems. Talk around the issues you have to resolve with each other and try and build a better picture of the other team's general working situation and the other issues they are facing.

If Swiss staff don't seem to have time to schedule going out for a meal or a drink (or their bosses think they don't have time), try arguing from the point of view of efficiency. Socialising will help you get to know each other better, so that you can work more efficiently together in the long term.

Long lunches to save time

Lorenz, a Swiss product manager told me he had been to Milan with his team for a day, trying to encourage his company's Italian plant to accept a plan designed by Swiss headquarters. He commented on the unsuccessful all-day meeting: 'They didn't seem to want to buy into it, but didn't really explain why'. I asked him how long his team had spent chatting informally with the Italian team, e.g. over lunch. He answered that he had scheduled a short lunch break, only 45 minutes, to save time. Maybe if lunch had lasted two or three hours, and his Swiss team had talked individually to different people on the Italian team, they would have found out more about why the Italians had problems with the plan. Some important information just doesn't come out in meetings, especially if it is related to internal power politics.

Chapter 26   Project team work

Involvement and independence

Jeannette is Swiss and works in Zurich for an IT company. She reports that her English colleagues work inefficiently:

> In our project management course at business school we learned that you make a plan, allocate tasks, consider resources, set milestones, and then everyone is free to work until the first milestone has been reached. If the planning is good, you can then work alone within a time-frame and are not dependent on each other. Our English colleagues do not work this way. It is very hard to pin them down. In a recent project we needed our English Technical Support team to define for us how they were going to go about a task. Instead of clearly defining their procedures and reporting to us 'Okay, we want to go about it this way', they kept getting different ideas, and were always talking again and changing their minds. At one point they had three different approaches in the same week. This means we couldn't leave them to get on with it but had to keep asking them for an update.

These differences in working styles can be partly accounted for by well-documented characteristics of US and German co-operation. According to Sylvia Schroll Machl,[58] a German psychologist, Germans and US employees have different interaction patterns in project team work. The German description has relevance to German Swiss work patterns and the American description to other Anglo-Saxon work patterns.

The German preference

* They like to make a thorough analysis of a problem in which team members contribute their expertise at the beginning.

* An analysis, once made and agreed upon, is firmly believed in and generally seen as definitive.

* After this very detailed analysis, all the team members know what is expected of them and set out to work independently without needing or wishing for much further communication until a further meeting is called to coordinate the results achieved by the team members individually.

The American preference

* They like to make a provisional analysis of a task, a much quicker setting of intermediate targets and a trial-and-error approach, co-ordinated by frequent spontaneous communication.

* Changes are readily made whenever a new strategy promises to give better results.

* Circumstances are expected to change and are taken into consideration throughout the project.

The differences Schroll Machl discovered are relevant to the perspectives of Jeannette and her English Technical Support colleagues. As is often the case in IT, the pioneer nature of the work they were doing meant that there were no established procedures. For her, the first task of Technical Support was to establish these, and then everyone would know where they were heading. For her English colleagues the first step was to try out a few things and see what worked.

Tom, an English scientist with children in Swiss school, pointed out that this difference begins in school, although it could be even earlier (see also chapter 12). Elizabeth, an English mother, added to this:
'The Swiss education system encourages you to follow a well-laid out procedure to get a guaranteed result. You will only obtain X if you do A, B, C then D. The British are less procedure focussed and more results focussed. You do all you have to do to get there. The objective has to be achieved, and how you go about it does not matter so much'.

Defining milestones

International Swiss companies with Anglo-American influence increasingly have a strong results focus. They are less likely to define A, B, C and D and then stick faithfully to the plan in order to reach the goal. The more management are of Anglo-Saxon origin, the more that flexibility will become part of the company culture. Marcel Trachsel of 'int-ext communications' works regularly with international project teams and recommends taking smaller steps in project work:

> Every time a group makes a decision, they have reached a milestone. They may be asking, 'Which direction are we now going in, and do we now take the blue or the yellow path?' The Anglos have a looser way of working, and are more willing to change their plans. Germanic decisions are more precise, and once you have written a project plan, it is written in stone. International project team leaders should plan smaller steps and define milestones more often. That means discussing things more often, and making decisions more often. A mono-cultural group does not need to do this.

Just brainstorming

According to Schroll Machl, an in-depth analysis with a definitive agreement for action is a feature of Germanic decision-making. However, as shown above, 'changing your mind' is common in international companies in German-speaking Switzerland. This working style may seem indecisive, disorganised and lacking direction to Swiss outside agencies and service providers. New staff members, German Swiss or German, may also be taken by surprise, as Rainer reports:

I moved from a well-known, traditional German company to a large international Swiss one. It took me some time to get used to the communication style of my new American boss, Tony, who was based in the States. We had a lot of phone contact in which he would make suggestions, like how to proceed with a project, and after I had taken steps to carry out his suggestions, for example by contacting people internally, he would phone with a different suggestion. I then had to phone internal colleagues back and say we had changed our minds.

Tony was apparently brainstorming, i.e. thinking aloud, and not imagining Rainer would act yet. People who knew him would wait until they were sure he had finished thinking through the issues before they took action. Rainer needed to start asking 'Would you like me to do something about this now, or do you want to think about it a bit more?' If Tony had actually been based in Switzerland, he might have been influenced by the more cautious Germanic communication style. Brainstorming is less popular in Switzerland than in the USA because it involves experimenting with ideas, and people feel they have to go through with what they have said. Hypothetical discussions are not popular.

Threats to independence

Both Jeannette and Rainer experienced a working style which involved more on-going liaison with colleagues or bosses than they were used to. Jeannette had to keep checking on the English support team to see how they were getting on. She would have preferred to have been given a description of exactly how they were going to proceed and be able to leave them to it. Similarly Rainer couldn't just go off and get on with the next step of the work. He needed to keep checking with Tony as to whether 'the plan' had changed.

For people who wish to work independently, the on-going involvement of others can seem like interference. When Thomas's Swiss telecommunications company started to take on foreign staff in the late 90s, he got a British boss and complained, 'She is always coming and interrupting us in our work, asking what we are doing. She can't just leave us to get on with it. Does she not trust us?' At this point the British boss was culturally exotic, and her way of working was clashing with the traditionally Swiss company culture, so it met with quite a bit of resistance.

Andreas, a Swiss banker, experienced the necessity of increased involvement with colleagues when he worked in London for two years. It was not always clear to him what he was supposed to be doing, and he assumed that with his less than perfect English he had missed something in the meetings. He felt embarrassed to go and ask people for more information. With time he realised that issues were in fact not being discussed thoroughly in meetings, but only a broad outline was being drawn. People were going to each other's desks to continue discussing details informally and then either letting the plan evolve further, or even turning it on its head. He had to break his habit of working independently, and instead approach his colleagues and start asking questions.

Swiss staff are often surprised by the Anglo-American expectation that a team will keep discussing its work once initial decisions have been made. The traditional Swiss preference for less communication in carrying out tasks reflects a desire to give people space or distance and not disturb their need for independence. The 'closed door' in some office buildings can be a symbol of this. Thomas's new boss may have come across like an interfering mother who didn't trust him to get on with the work on his own. At first Andreas may have felt very dependent having to go and ask colleagues for help.

In English-speaking countries, staff usually expect and want this ongoing involvement or interfacing with their colleagues as they complete a task. They are less likely to be specialists in a particular field than their Germanic counterparts and more often learn from others on-the-job. They get the information they need by asking the right people, rather than by working it out alone. (See also chapters 12 and 13 for possible parallels with interaction and independence in early childhood in Switzerland and English-speaking countries).

Figuring it out by yourself

At university, the different attitudes to interaction show up too. According to the magazine *Swiss News*,[53] ETH (The Federal Technical University in Zurich) Jürg Dual, a Swiss professor who has also taught mechanics to undergraduates at Cornell University in New York, considers Swiss students to be better at abstract thinking than their American counterparts:

"My American students made it clear that they expected me to show them step-by-step how to solve their homework problems. In Switzerland the students figure out how to solve the problems by themselves."

In some practical situations there are advantages to students not solving problems by themselves. John is a British student of engineering at a Swiss university. He describes his experience of team work among students as follows:

> Swiss students do what they have to do well, but they don't take responsibility for others' tasks. If they believe what they are doing is perfectly logical, they don't see a need to communicate about it. I saw this in an engineering device-making project for which we had three related teams: A, the students ordering materials, B, the students in charge of the machine shop where the work was done, and C, the students who were assembling the devices. A ordered a part for C and had it sent to B at the standard delivery address used by suppliers. When it arrived, B did not know what it was for, and threw it away. C waited for it in vain, then complained to A that it hadn't come. A said, 'We had it sent to B'. When B was asked why they had thrown it away, they said, 'It wasn't for us. It's not our problem'.

One of the main aims of this project was to give the students their first experience of working in teams. Opinions could vary as to what kind of improvements need to be made if a company is in this type of situation. John's opinion was that the teams needed more spontaneous communication, along the lines of the village market. Alternatively, in the well-oiled machine model, different tasks might remain compartmentalised but staff might improve their procedures with inbuilt rules (e.g., don't throw anything away) if something unexpected arrived.

Horst is in pharmaceutical production in a large pharmaceutical company and assures me that the cellars of their buildings are full of mysterious materials which lie around for years, but no one dares throw them away, including some hose pipes valued at Fr. 400,000. In a village market culture, people would be more likely to ask around to see who ordered it.

Future prospects in Switzerland

Short-term task-based projects with a large contingent of foreigners involved are becoming more typical in Switzerland, and are set up for the duration of one particular project (which may succeed or fail). Staff move around a lot within the company, working on one project after another, and some staff leave the company completely if their project does not work out.

The kind of relationships people have at work bring us back to the peach and the coconut described in chapter one. Peach relationships are often more short-term, and people start getting to know each other pretty quickly. In coconut relationships you take it slowly, and need more time to open up to people.

Christian is a Swiss project manager who has worked for a small Swiss company and now works for IBM. He sees the short-term project model as a trend which will have a great influence on the Swiss way of building business relationships.

In terms of business relationships, the younger generation has nothing in common with their parents. The idea of a sense of obligation between the employer and employees is completely breaking up. It used to be that someone who left the company was a traitor, because it was like a kind of family. Nowadays business relationships are short term, with people working together in projects for only 6-12 months. The focus is business only, with the start and end points visible and known, and bonuses linked to that goal. There is only a short preparation time before starting the job. Swiss people now have to learn a lot about building relationships quickly, e.g. building a foundation in which people can trust you. This new short-term focus will change the way we define relationships.

After the party

The party is over but the discussion has just begun. There are so many more stories which can be told by people who live on the interface between cultures, and each one is unique. The linguistic anthropologist Michael Agar believes a 'good story' introduces an idea about culture better than an abstract academic essay and that when we go and live in a new culture, we can all be 'participant observers' of the world we engage in:

> You jump in and do everyday life with people to get a first-hand feel for how things go. At the same time, you keep a third eye at an altitude of several feet above the action and watch what's going on in a more distant way.[59]

I hope the stories and ideas shared by participant observers have given you food for thought as you 'jump in and do everyday life' and then share your perspectives with your Swiss or foreign partner, friends, relatives, colleagues and neighbours.

This book was very clearly a joint effort, although I take full responsibility for the final product. I greatly appreciated the contributions, support, wisdom and good will of many people, Swiss and foreign, as I compiled material for this book, and I would like to thank them all here: Ariane Curdy, Professor Dan Daniels, Dr

Rolf Keller, Martin Wacker, Natalie Corman, Dr Markus Wartmann, Dr Geoffrey Myers, Regula Graf, Dr Stefan Fischer, Darlene Grieder, Valerie Walder, Eileen, Sarah Nevill, Dr Peter Hungerford, Dr Werner Stöcklin, Dr Nils Blom, Nicole M, Leslie Guggiari, Alain de Botton, Dr Annelise Ermer, Kelley Veer, Rosemary, Monika, Ellen Baumgartner, Erik Fuller-Lewis, Lucy, Sharon Dreyfus, Sandra Naehrig, Joyce, Jean Turner, Christine Wenk, Sue, Pat Robins, Ralf Woelfle, Emma, Karin, Dr Siegfried Schmitt, Kathrin, Sally, Anita, Dr Lawrence Desmond, Beat, Paolo, Dr Marcel Trachsel, Christine Obrecht, Dr Torsten Reimer, Catherine Shultis, Dr Kenneth McRitchie, Steve Pawlett, Dr Urs Späti, Andrea Fischer, Tanya, Jean Darling, Chip Darling, Janice, Max, Sam, June, Jane Christ, Olivia, Heinz, Mary, John, Dr Valerie Fowler, Deborah Schüpbach, Vreni B, Dr Jakob Christ, Ursula Stampfli, Walter Stampfli, Lili Haefliger, Corinne, Wendy Schmitt, Dr Helen McRitchie, Graham Tritt, Dr Roger Dreyfus, Margaretha Hall-Debrunner, Rudolf, Beat Kernen, Hans Oertig, Dr Ulrike Hoffmann-Richter, Dr Paul Parin, Dr Albert Debrunner, Birgit, Catherine T, Esther Kubli, Irene M, Yannis, Lila Buchs, Paul Cray, Armin Zacher, Christoph Krähenbühl, Mary Blom, Heidi, Didier, Roger Bonner, Sandy, Sabine, Ulrich Rubli, Charlie, Rolf, André, Christoph Meier, Professor Walter Dettling, Wendy Richardson, Debby, Klaus, Carlo, Fabio, Frank, Doris, Vivian, Dr Petra Schubert, Matthias, Sharon Dreyfus, Christian, Claudine, Marla, Claudia, Annette, Laurence, Dr Marcel Oertig, Gottfried, Joanne, Sylvia, Peter, Anne-Louise Bornstein, Annemarie Pfeifer, Lorenz, Jeannette, Tom, Elizabeth Holman, Rainer, Thomas, Andreas, John and last but not least, Christian with his prophetic words at the end of the book. It was impossible to quote all the insights I gleaned, but they were all very valuable and all have influenced the general direction of the book. There were many more topics raised, waiting to be discussed, but that's another party.

The seeds for this project were sown during many stimulating discussions over the last 15 years, which got me thinking about cultural issues. I would particularly like to thank my husband Hans, Alex Scholtz, Debby Gysin, Natalie Corman, Liz Tighe, Jane Christ, Mary Blom, Nina Meier-Bradlin and Val Fowler for their valuable insights down the years. Thanks also go to the participants of my English classes and intercultural training seminars who shared their perspectives on their various cultures over the years, and provided me with continuous opportunities for learning.

Special thanks go to Dr Dan Daniels and Wendy Zimmermann for their detailed editorial input on the text, and also to Dr. Torsten Reimer, Dr Laurence Desmond, Christine Wenk, Ursula Stampfli, Mary Blom and Alexandra Scholtz for their helpful comments on various drafts, and to Carol Siegenthaler for proof-reading.

Many thanks also go to Dianne Dicks for being a positive, patient, hard-working and extremely flexible publisher and to Professor Richard Fay, my tutor at Manchester University for introducing me to many intercultural concepts to broaden my horizon.

I could not have written this book without the encouragement of my family. Hans, my husband was, as always, extremely supportive, and my daughters Sarah and Fiona encouraged me not to work too hard. I also appreciated the wisdom of perceptive friends and family in Scotland, in particular, Lesley Donaldson, Anne Cusack and my mother, Betty Davidson.

Appendix: Historical reasons for politeness

Chapter 3 described German Swiss preferring to either express
themselves directly or remain silent. Why is this kind of polite in-
directness not valued much? The German expression for politeness, *Höflichkeit,* comes from the German word *Hof*, meaning the
court of royalty or nobles. In this sense it is similar to the English
word 'courtesy' taken from French, from the word court. The modern English word 'politeness' is close to the French, *politesse* and
was originally connected with politics and power, e.g. how to behave or speak appropriately in order to get on with people who
have power over you, and not risk provoking their anger. Offend-
ing a king may have resulted in getting your head chopped off. As
Switzerland has never had a royal family, and the Swiss confed-
eration was set up to escape the power of princes in the surrounding regions, it could be argued that they have not had much use for
politeness in the sense of kowtowing those in power. There was
always a sense that everyone should be of equal status and should
be able to speak to everyone else in the same down-to-earth way.
Even words like 'Madam' cannot be translated adequately into
Swiss German.

Etiquette as a duty

In Germany there was a trend to criticise politeness in the 18th century, even though they had an Emperor and many princes who held court. Knigge, the most famous etiquette expert in the German-speaking world in the 18th century, was critical of 'conventional politeness' (i.e. using polite expressions). He believed that the rules for behaviour should be founded on the *'teaching of duties, which we owe to all types of people, und in turn can demand of them'*.[60] This fits well with the view that *Anstand* or correct behaviour is a must while politeness is an extra. The Grimm brothers, the writers of fairy tales, were also linguists and wrote an article in which they contrasted 'crafty or clever politeness' with modesty. Clever politeness is aimed at being rewarded while modesty aims at truth and authenticity.

Notes

1. It was beyond the scope of this book to explore a wider range of cultural differences experienced by English speakers from other cultures, e.g. from Asian and African countries. This would be a book in itself, looking at a wide range of communication patterns (e.g. body language) , approaches to family (respect for older people), attitudes to time, etc.

2. www.culture-relations.ch.

3. K. O'Sullivan, *Understanding Ways: Communicating Between Cultures*, Hale and Iremonger (1994).

4. Kurt Lewin, *Field Theory in Social Science*, New York Harper (1951). Lewin's ideas were developed by Fons Trompenaars into specific and diffuse cultures. Quoted in C. Hampden-Turner and F. Trompenaars, *Building Cross-cultural Competence,* Nicholas Brealey Publishing (1993). The peach and the coconut idea are reported to have come from the trainers Goldstein, Robins, McDonald and Waldmann of US Communication Consultants.

5. Put simply, accent is the way people pronounce the words while dialect also involves consistently using different words and grammar.

6. Website: http://survey2000.nationalgeographic.com.

7. Swiss Federal Statistical Office www.statistik.admin.ch (Bundesamt für Statistik). These mobility statistics are taken from the 1990 census. Results from the 2000 census are available from 2003. It is thought that people in Switzerland began to commute longer distances in the 1990s, rather than move house. Improved intercity train connections (e.g. St Gallen, Zurich, Biel, Geneva) made the commute easier.

8. See note 7.

9. P. Brown and S. Levinson, *Politeness* (1987). Brown and Levinson use the terminology 'face wants'.

10. R. Scollon and S. Wong Scollon, *Intercultural Communication,* Blackwell (1995).

11. See note 9.

12. L.R. Mao, *Beyond Politeness Theory: 'Face' revisited and renewed.* In *Journal of Pragmatics* 21, 451-486.

13. Thanks to Tom, who first described this ritual verbal exchange as a dance.

14. Distribution of languages: German 63,3%, French 19.2%, Italian 7.6 %, Romansh 0.6%, others 8.9% (=of foreign origin). German-speaking cantons: BS/BL, SO, AG, LU, GL, ZG, SZ, ZH, TG, SH, SG, AI/AR, NW/OW. Four French speaking cantons: GE, VD, NE, JU. Three bilingual G/F cantons: BE, FE, VS. One Italian speaking canton: TI. One canton with three languages G/I/R: GR.

15. Martin Stauffer, *Fremdsprachen an Schweizer Schulen*, in R. Watts, and H. Murray (Ed), *Die fünfte Landessprache? Englisch in der Schweiz,* (v/d/f 2001).

16. Stauffer, see note 15.

17. Heather Murray, *Englisch als Wissenschaftssprach an der Universität Bern*, in Watts and Murray, see note 15.

18. The Flemish write standard Dutch and speak with varying degrees of dialect. I learnt standard Dutch, which was accepted by the Flemish as Flemish. In Switzerland the difference is much clearer, and if you speak High German in Switzerland no one will refer to it as Swiss German (except visiting Germans).

19. Paul Parin and Goldy Parin-Matthey, Zurich, *Typische Unterschiede zwischen Schweizern und Süddeutschen aus dem gebildeten Kleinbürgertum* in *Psyche*, Heft 11-XXX (1976).

20. Bill Bryson, *Mother Tongue,* Penguin Books (1990).

21. Peter Habicht, *Lifting the Mask; your guide to Basel Fasnacht*, Bergli Books (2001).

22. *NZZ Folio* June 2001.

23. Jakob Christ, *Erlebte Sozialpsychiatrie - Amerikanische Anfänge und Europäische Traditionen,* Psychiatrie Verlag, Edition das Narrenschiff (2002).

24. *Das Magazin* no 31, 2001.

25. *Facts,* 8 November 2001.

26. Shawne Fielding, the flamboyant wife of Thomas Borer, Swiss diplomat in Berlin, also provoked many letters to the newspapers every time she made a public appearance. Some people thought she was terrible for Switzerland's image and others thought she was great.

27. There is an expression 'more Swiss than the Swiss' to describe foreigners who have lived a while in Switzerland and take the rules very much to heart.

28. See note 19.

29. H. R. Markus and S. Kitayama, *Culture and the Self: Implications for Cognition, Emotion and Motivation, Psychological Review*, 98 (2), 224-253.

30. Remo Largo, *Kinderjahre,* Piper (2000).

31. Shakuntala Devi, *Awaken the Genius in Your Child*, Element Books (1999).

32. J. Tobin, D. Wu and Dana H. Davidson, *Preschool in Three Cultures,* Japan, China and the United States, Yale University Press (1989).

33. Campaign organised by the Polizeikonkordats Nordwestschweiz.

34. State of Geneva website (in French): www.familles-ge.ch.

35. *Swiss News* 3/2001.

36. *Basler Zeitung*, 13 August 2001.

37. *Basler Zeitung,* 1 December 2001, *Sprachschulen: So bringen Sie sich sprachlich richtig auf Kurs.*

38. Daniel Stotz, quoting Andreas Troppan in *Sprachpolitik und Sprachpraxis in 'big business': Der Status des Englischen*, in Watts and Murray, see note 15.

39. Ulla Kleinberger Günther, *Sprachliche Höflichkeit in innerbetrieblichen E-mails* in H. H. Lüger (Ed), *Höflichkeitsstile*, Peter Lang (2001).

40. *Tabu,* Kantonsmuseum Baselland, Liestal (2001).

41. Schubert, Wölfle and Dettling (Ed), *Fulfillment im E-Business,* Hanser (2001).

42. See note 39.

43. See also Lucia Bleuler and Ulrich Weber, *Knigge für Leute von heute*, AT Verlag (2001).

44. *Pons Collins English German Dictionary* (1997).

45. *Bilanz*, February 2001, *Fragen hilft weiter.*

46. *Handelszeitung* nr 50, 12 Dec. 2001, *Leichte Worte mit Gewicht.*

47. This book by Don Gabor has a very peachy title: *How to Start a Conversation and Make Friends,* Simon and Schuster (1983).

48. *Handelszeitung* nr 9, 28 Feb. 2001, *Schrecklich zwanglos.*

49. *Facts* no 26, 2001.

50. Demoscope, Research and Marketing, Adligenswil.

51. Geert Hofstede, *Culture's Consequences,* Sage (1984).

52. Elisabeth Gehrer, Minister of Education, Science and Culture, Austria, on a visit to Basel University to discuss leadership, quoted in the *Basler Zeitung,* 20 Oct. 2001, *Basel als Vorbild für Österreich.*

53. Extract from a document in English by the Schweizerische Konferenz der kantonalen Erziehungsdirektoren, Bern (2001). Website www.unibe.ch/e/eurydice/eury.

54. *Das Magazin*, 2000.

55. *Basler Zeitung*, 9 June 2001. Profesor Baitsch is responsible for Organisation and Management at the Institute of Applied Psychology (IAP) in Zurich.

56. *Cash* no 39, 28 Sept 2001, *Die alte Garde ist weg, wer rückt nach?* Five prize winning top managers were given an award by *Cash*, in conjunction with the Gottlieb Duttweiler Institute (GDI). David Bosshart is Managing Director of the GDI.

57. English: We'll do it, we're going to do it, we are doing it, we do it, we will be doing it, we'll have done it. Swiss German: *mir machen es, mir werden es mache.*

58. Sylvia Schroll-Machl, *Kulturbedingte Unterschiede im Problemlöseprozess bei deutsch-amerikanischen Arbeitsgruppen*, in Alexander Thomas, *Psychologie Interkulturellen Handelns* (1996). Preferences summarised in English by Henri de Jongste, *Dutch and German business cultures and their impact on communication with British business partners* in *Language and Intercultural Training*, Vol 16, No 1 (1998).

59. Michael Agar, *Language Shock*, Quill (1994).

60. Knigge, *Über den Umgang mit Menschen* (1790).

Index

A

About the author

Margaret Oertig-Davidson is Scottish and has lived and worked in Switzerland since 1987, training business and professional people to communicate internationally. She has developed and conducted a range of cross-cultural seminars for international companies and universities, with a main focus on business relations between Swiss and English-speaking cultures. She lives near Basel with her Swiss husband and two daughters.

About Bergli Books

Bergli Books publishes, promotes and distributes books in English that focus on travel, on living in Switzerland and on intercultural matters:

Ticking Along with the Swiss, edited by Dianne Dicks, entertaining and informative personal experiences of many 'foreigners' living in Switzerland. ISBN 3-9520002-4-8.

Ticking Along Too, edited by Dianne Dicks, has more personal experiences, a mix of social commentary, warm admiration and observations of the Swiss as friends, neighbors and business partners. ISBN 3-9520002-1-3.

Ticking Along Free, edited by Dianne Dicks, with more stories about living with the Swiss, this time with also some prominent Swiss writers. ISBN 3-905252-02-3

Ticking Along on Tape, a 60-minute audio cassette with a selection of ten readings from *Ticking Along with the Swiss* and *Ticking Along Too*. ISBN 3-905252-00-7.

Cupid's Wild Arrows; intercultural romance and its consequences, edited by Dianne Dicks, contains personal experiences of 55 authors living with two worlds in one partnership. ISBN 3-9520002-2-1.

Laughing Along with the Swiss by Paul Bilton has everything you need to know to endear you to the Swiss forever. ISBN 3-905252-01-5.

A Taste of Switzerland, by Sue Style, with over 50 recipes that show the richness of this country's diverse gastronomic cultures. ISBN 3-9520002-7-2.

The Surprising Wines of Switzerland, *a practical guide to Switzerland's best kept secret*, by John C. Sloan, an objective and comprehensive description of Swiss wines. ISBN 3-9520002-6-4.

Inside Outlandish, by Susan Tuttle, illustrated by ANNA, a collection of essays that takes you to the heart of feeling at home in strange, new places. ISBN 3-9520002-8-0.

Berne; a portrait of Switzerland's federal capital, of its people, culture and spirit, by Peter Studer (photographs), Walter Däpp, Bernhard Giger and Peter Krebs. ISBN 3-9520002-9-9.

Red Benches and others; *a journal/notebook for your viewpoints*, with photography of benches throughout Switzerland by Clive Minnitt and Frimmel Smith and blank pages for your notes. ISBN 3-905252-08-2.

Lifting the Mask; *your guide to Basel Fasnacht* by Peter Habicht, illustrations by Fredy Prack. ISBN 3-905252-04-X.

Once Upon an Alp by Eugene V. Epstein. A selection of the best stories from this well-known American/Swiss humorist ISBN 3-905252-05-8.

Swiss Me by Roger Bonner, illustrations by Edi Barth. Playful essays and stories about becoming Swiss. ISBN 3-905252-11-2.

Culture Smart! Switzerland by Kendall Maycock. A guide to customs and etiquette for doing business with the Swiss. ISBN 3-905252-12-0.

Hoi – your Swiss German survival guide by Sergio J. Lievano and Nicole Egger. Have fun learning Swiss dialect with 200 cartoons and over 2000 words and phrases, including a Swiss German to English and an English to Swiss German dictionary. ISBN 3-905252-13-9.

Ask for a catalog or visit www.bergli.ch.

Dear Reader,
Your opinion can help us. We would like to know what you think of *Beyond Chocolate*.
Where did you learn about this book?

Had you heard about Bergli Books before reading this book?
What did you enjoy about this book?

Any criticism?

If you teach English, would you like to receive some tips for using this book in your classroom?

Would you like to receive more information about the books we publish and distribute? If so, please give us your name and address and we'll send you a catalogue.
Name:
Address:
City/Country:

Cut out page, fold here, staple and mail to:

Bergli Books
Rümelinsplatz 19
CH-4001 Basel
Switzerland